MANAGING HYPERTENSI

MANAGING HYPERTENSION

John Dick BSc MBChB FRCP(Ed)
Consultant Physician and Honorary Senior Lecturer in Medicine,
Ninewells Hospital and Medical School, Dundee, Scotland

ALTMAN

Published by Altman Publishing, 7 Ash Copse, Bricket Wood, St Albans, Herts, AL2 3YA

First edition 2007

Typeset in 10/12.5 Optima by Phoenix Photosetting, Chatham, Kent
Printed in Great Britain by Chiltern Printers (Slough) Ltd

ISBN 13: 978-1-86036-043-5

A catalogue record for this book is available from the British Library

∞ Printed on acid-free text paper, manufactured in accordance with ANSI/NISO Z39.48-1992 (Permanence of Paper)

CONTENTS

ABOUT THE AUTHOR

John Dick is a Consultant Physician and Honorary Senior Lecturer in Medicine at Ninewells Hospital and Medical School, Dundee. He trained in medicine and in chemical pathology, and is a consultant in the Vascular Team. Together with colleagues, he runs the Cardiovascular Risk Clinic, a combined hypertension, lipids and risk assessment clinic. He recently reviewed hypertension as the lead contributor for this chapter in the updated SIGN Guidelines. His research interests are in global risk, atherothrombosis and patterns of blood flow.

PREFACE

There is a famous picture of Churchill, Roosevelt and Stalin at Yalta during the Second World War. All three went on to die of the consequences of hypertension, which at the time was virtually untreatable. (Roosevelt's personal physician prescribed a diet and a reduction in stress.) The few drugs that were available were widely regarded as being worse than the disease itself. Moving forward a decade or two, the condition was more recognised for its lethal consequences, but the drugs had hardly advanced. Individuals were not referred, far less treated, unless there was severe disease, often manifest by end-organ damage. The use of drugs was dictated by hospital practitioners, who would investigate with intravenous urograms, and wind up prescribing rauwolfia alkaloids, notorious for inducing depression. Compliance was an issue, to say the least. But, beginning in the 1960s, newer and better tolerated drugs began to alter the prospects of the hypertensive patient, and with better adherence came a widening of the net, with physicians more willing and better able to control hypertension before the onset of more established disease.

Hypertension has now moved from the province of the specialist, through various clinical incarnations, to being a matter for routine management in the primary care setting. More and more individuals have their blood pressure checked in everyday life, for interest, family history, or the more prosaic reasons of health and property insurances and mortgages. Health-care professionals are faced with an epidemic of cardiovascular disease, and health-care provision has to factor in the huge cost of prescribing, not just for those with overt disease, but also as prophylaxis. There is a huge forest of literature. Why add to this?

With the advent of the General Medical Services contract, its inherent cardiovascular risk targets, and the second version of the Joint British Societies' Guidelines on Prevention of Cardiovascular Disease in Clinical Practice, health care in the United Kingdom is taking on the challenge of managing and reducing the burden of cardiovascular disease. This is, in effect, a public health initiative of ground-breaking proportions.

This short book is not aimed at academics, nor does it pretend to any comprehensive overview of the subject. Instead, its purpose is to provide a succinct account of hypertension and its practical management. It should be seen as an adjunct to published guidelines, with concise advice, and the tripwires for onward referral. Key points are contained in summary blocks, and there is an advanced reading list at the end of each chapter. Above all, busy practitioners should be able to find the help that they require without having to search reams of references and documents.

JD
March 2007

ABBREVIATIONS

ABPM	ambulatory blood pressure monitoring
ACE	angiotensin converting enzyme
ACEI	angiotensin converting enzyme inhibitor
ANP	atrial natriuretic peptide
ARB	angiotensin receptor blocker
ASCOT	Anglo-Scottish Cardiovascular Outcomes Trial
ATI, ATII	angiotensin I, II
BMI	body mass index
BP	blood pressure
CB1	cannabinoid type 1 receptor
CCBD	calcium channel blocking drug
CHD	coronary heart disease
CK	creatine kinase
COPD	chronic obstructive pulmonary disease
CVA	cerebrovascular accident
CVD	cardiovascular disease
ECG	electrocardiogram
eGFR	estimated glomerular filtration rate
FBC	full blood count
FMD	fibromuscular dysplasia
GFR	glomerular filtration rate
GGT	gamma-glutamyltransferase
GLP1	glucagon-like peptide 1
HDL	high density lipoprotein
5HIAA	5-hydroxyindolacetic acid
HRT	hormone replacement therapy
IHD	ischaemic heart disease
ISH	isolated systolic hypertension
IUGR	intrauterine growth retardation
IVU	intravenous urogram

JBS1, JBS2	Joint British Societies' Guidelines on Prevention of Cardiovascular Disease in Clinical Practice
JGA	juxtaglomerular apparatus
LDL	low density lipoprotein
LFT	liver function test
LVH	left ventricular hypertrophy
MI	myocardial infarction
MRFIT	The Multiple Risk Factor Intervention Trial
NRT	nicotine replacement therapy
OCP	oral contraceptive pill
PAD	peripheral arterial disease
PPI	protein pump inhibitor
PV	plasma viscosity
RAAS	renin–angiotensin–aldosterone system
SCORE	Systematic Coronary Risk Evaluation
SIGN	Scottish Intercollegiate Guideline Network
TIA	transient ischaemic attack
tPA	tissue plasminogen activator
TSH	thyroid-stimulating hormone
UKPDS	UK Prospective Diabetes Study
U/Es	urea and electrolytes
WHO	World Health Organization

1 INTRODUCTION

We are all hypertensive. Compared to hunter-gatherer man, we all have a high blood pressure, and this rises inexorably with age. The decision to grade a particular level of blood pressure as pathological is therefore dependent upon societies' appreciation of risk, the medical consequences of therapy (good and bad), and the health economics of delivering antihypertensive therapy, versus not delivering. The pragmatic definition adopted in many guidelines cannot be bettered: 'the level of blood pressure at which there is evidence that blood pressure reduction does more good than harm.' Newer, cleaner drugs have moved the goalposts, as have newer epidemiological and interventional studies, and a changing public health background.

Cause or consequence, with senescence our arteries become less compliant. Hypertension produces thickening of the medial layers of the blood vessel walls, with direct pathological consequences (including occlusion), and is also a major contributor to more generalised atherothrombosis, presumably by damaging the intimal lining of the arteries. The effects of hypertension on specific organs and tissues, known as end-organ damage, are due to a combination of these two effects. Glomerular damage in the kidney, small vessel damage in the brain, and retinal damage all reflect this pathology. In the heart, the strain of pumping against a high resistance pressure produces left ventricular hypertrophy; untreated, this in turn causes the heart muscle to exceed its available blood supply, resulting in myocardial infarction, or more insidious cardiomyopathy and left ventricular failure.

The coexistence of other pathologies that damage blood vessels, such as smoking, hyperlipidaemia and diabetes, all dramatically worsen these processes. In terms of risk calculation, they are multiplicative rather than additive.

Of the family of cardiovascular diseases – cerebrovascular, peripheral vascular and cardiac – hypertension correlates most tightly with stroke. About 80% of strokes in the UK are thromboembolic, and a further 10%

are haemorrhagic. Persisting hypertension after a cerebrovascular event is a very strong predictor of repeat events and of other cardiovascular disease. The health economics of cerebrovascular disease are truly awful, ranging from productive work days lost to long-term hospital care.

Clinical case

A 74-year-old lady was referred to the clinic with refractory blood pressure. This was confirmed by ambulatory monitoring, with a daytime mean of 185/110 mmHg. On discussion she produced an extensive list of side-effects with all first-line antihypertensives. Two other drugs were suggested and tried. She returned to the clinic requesting a drug holiday, insisting that she felt much better off medication. After a long discussion, the clinic doctor acquiesced. Four weeks later, prior to review, she presented with an acute right middle cerebral artery thrombotic stroke. She made a modest functional recovery, and lost her independence as a result, requiring placement in a residential home. She restarted one of the original antihypertensives (an ACE inhibitor), with no subsequent problems.

There is no criticism intended here, either of the patient or of the reviewing doctor, but a clear understanding of the risks and benefits may have induced a different outcome. In addition, although I am in favour of always trying to find a drug regimen that suits the individual, I suspect that an oscillating blood pressure with on–off treatment may be actively detrimental.

Target organ damage isn't always clinically obvious. Catastrophic ocular events are outnumbered by insidious cardiac and renal consequences.

Clinical case

A 46-year-old oil industry maintenance worker was referred after a routine medical to go abroad. He had last worked offshore 5 years previously, at which time he had borderline hypertension. He had held a number of different posts for changing employers over the intervening years, and five different general practitioner registra-

---

tions. On referral, his BP was confirmed at 210/115 mmHg, and he had grade 3 retinopathy, ECG voltage hypertrophy, proteinuria and an estimated glomerular filtration rate (eGFR) of 27. Renal ultrasound showed small kidneys. Aggressive blood pressure intervention has arrested his renal decline for now, and he is reviewed by the renal team in the 'low clearance' clinic. He cannot work offshore, and is aware that he is likely to require renal replacement therapy.

Again there is no criticism intended, with this man's peripatetic lifestyle the main cause for this unfortunate presentation. Many uncontrolled hypertensives avoid this renal outcome. The significance is in the lack of symptomatology until a relatively end-stage picture had developed.

Clinical case

A 62-year-old retired PE teacher presented as an emergency with acute left ventricular failure. This responded to diuretics and an ACE inhibitor. He had a 10-year history of prior hypertension, and was referred to the clinic for follow-up. At review, he revealed that he had disliked the effort-limiting side-effects of his previous β-blocker therapy, and so had taken his medication for only a few days prior to each appointment with his family doctor.

The main problem here was of communication between this man and his doctor. As above, this man was astounded at the apparent disconnect between the severity of his cardiac damage and his lack of symptoms right up to the point of presentation.

These three cases have all been seen in the clinic within the past year, and demonstrate the potential for catastrophic outcome for missed or untreated hypertension. In addition, the 'rule of halves', first proposed 30 years ago, has been borne out by subsequent studies. Half of all hypertensives are undiagnosed; half of those diagnosed are untreated; half of those treated are uncontrolled. This means that only 12.5% of hypertensives are actually managed to target. The public health message from this is clear.

The epidemiology of hypertension is that blood pressure is distributed in any given population as a classical bell-shaped curve (Figure 1.1). Just as for cholesterol, the decision to call one individual normal and his/her neighbour hypertensive is to impose cut-points upon an essentially continuous biological distribution curve. There is no doubt regarding those at high risk, nor even those at moderate risk, especially when calculated as

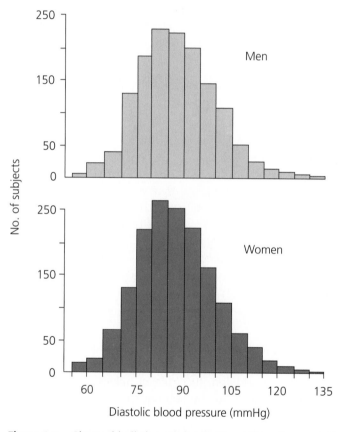

Figure 1.1 Classical bell-shaped distribution of blood pressure in a population. Reproduced with permission from Hawthorne VM, Greaves DA, Beevers DG. (1974) *BMJ* **3**: 600–603.

a global risk score. But the cut-points for intervention or otherwise are dictated not just by medical outcomes, but by health economics (Figure 1.2). Lowering the mean population blood pressure by 12/6 mmHg would reduce stroke incidence by 40% and heart attack by 25%. This is because the majority of events still occur in those at modest risk, which in turn is because this group forms the vast majority of individuals. The cost implications of this are considerable, with the gains offset by a decade or more. The more compelling evidence from recent trials, the effective reduction in the cost of various medications, and a growing public awareness have triggered a public health initiative to take this forward.

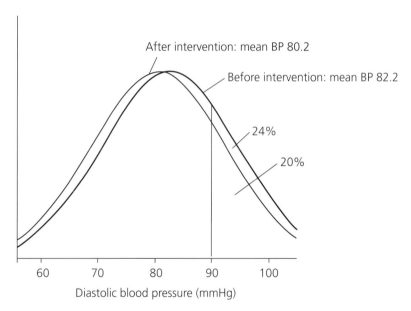

Diastolic blood pressure (mmHg)

Figure 1.2 A population-based intervention strategy among men and women aged 35 to 65 years of all races combined. Before intervention, 24% of the population had a mean diastolic BP above 90 mmHg whereas after intervention this figure had fallen to 20%. Reproduced with permission from Cook NR, Cohen J, Hebert PR, Taylor JO, Hennekens CH. (1995) *Arch Intern Med* **155**: 701–709.

Key points

- All adults in westernised societies tend towards hypertension with increasing age.
- Effective treatment has a large impact upon cardiovascular risk.
- Hypertensive damage is insidious and cumulative.
- Clinical endpoints from hypertensive damage are often catastrophic.
- Hypertension is an important part of the pathophysiology of atherosclerosis, and must be considered within the context of global risk.
- Population studies are unequivocal in their support for screening and intervention for hypertension and global risk.

References and further reading

Cook NR, Cohen J, Hebert PR, Taylor J, Hennekens CH. (1995) Implications of small reductions in diastolic blood pressure for primary prevention. *Arch Int Med* **155**: 701–709.

Hawthorne VM, Greaves DA, Beevers DG. (1974) Blood pressure in a Scottish town. *BMJ* **3,** 600–603.

Smith WCS, Lee AJ, Crombie IK, Tunstall-Pedoe H. (1990) Control of blood pressure in Scotland; the rule of halves. *BMJ* **300,** 981–983.

2   HISTORY

The relationship between hypertension and early mortality can be traced back to Chinese physicians some 4000 years ago, who noted more rigid, bounding pulses in individuals with a high salt intake, and associated this with early death. In the more modern age, the Society of Actuaries Study published in 1939 showed increasing cardiovascular mortality with rising quintiles of both systolic and diastolic blood pressure. Similar life insurance data was published in the early 1960s. But the two most significant studies relating hypertension to cardiovascular risk are the Framingham study, and The Multiple Risk Factor Intervention Trial (MRFIT). Both of these studies placed hypertension in the context of global cardiovascular risk.

Framingham is a small dormitory town to the west of Boston, chosen for study because of its stable population, and the direct rail link with the city, which enabled an easy commute for the investigators. Most modern risk calculations are derived at least in part from the Framingham equations produced from this study. No interventions were used, but starting in the 1940s a huge database was built up regarding smoking, cholesterol, blood pressure, glucose tolerance and ECG patterns, using the last of these to detect left ventricular hypertrophy (LVH). Although the original study was aimed at coronary heart disease, the more general cardiovascular risk has since been computed, with the addition of stroke the major difference. There is a significant gradation of risk and event rate with increase in blood pressure, and a significant multiplication of risk with other risk factors. The Framingham data and equation provide the basis for most risk scoring systems in current use.

The MRFIT screened 356 222 men for cholesterol, blood pressure and smoking. The follow-up data on these screenees showed the synergistic effect of these three risk factors. The effect is so powerful that this gave rise to the concept that intervention should not be aimed at a single risk factor alone. Global risk must always be considered and all relevant risk factors dealt with where possible.

So the risk of cardiovascular disease is directly and continuously related to blood pressure. Stroke, coronary heart disease (CHD), heart failure, renal impairment and cognitive decline are all affected. A decision to regard a point on this continuum as indicative of a disease is dictated by society and health economics. Taking 140/90 mmHg as a cut-point, for example, grades 4% of the under-30s as hypertensive, rising to more than 80% of the over 80s. The critical question, therefore, is does intervening produce health benefit?

As alluded to in the preface, the early drugs for hypertension were extremely unpleasant. They were not routinely used except for malignant hypertension, where the alternative was a shut-ended prognosis. Studies published in the 1950s and early 1960s showed the untreated prognosis of accelerated hypertension to be 80% mortality at 2 years; this was converted to 85% 5-year survival with these drugs. The question of treatment was thus answered in principle. The issue became one of finding a level for intervention commensurate with the cost and side-effect profile of the drugs. As the 1960s progressed, it was accepted that placebo-controlled trials in patients with diastolic pressures of greater than 110 were no longer ethical. Trials were conducted in what would now be regarded as mild to moderate hypertension, in asymptomatic individuals. Large-scale trial design was in its infancy, leading to some anomalies from inadequate run-in periods, incorrect drug doses, and low event rates in the control groups. By the early 1980s, a clear reduction in stroke events had been proven and seemed independent of the agents used. The effect on cardiac disease was less clear, as were the indications in specific groups, such as diabetics, the elderly, and those with isolated systolic hypertension.

The last two decades have seen a number of well-designed randomised controlled trials which have answered many of the remaining questions. Diabetics benefit from blood pressure lowering, and should have lower targets than the general population. The elderly benefit from antihypertensive therapy, particularly in stroke reduction. Blood pressure lowering reduces cardiac as well as cerebral events. Isolated systolic hypertension should be treated. There is no J-shaped curve, that is, no reasonably achievable threshold effect below which lowering blood pressure becomes detrimental. Aspirin reduces stroke risk further. Lipid lowering is mandated as part of global risk management, and reduces risk further still.

Post-stroke, blood pressure lowering produces an additional reduction in second cardiovascular events.

The remaining questions are concerned with the choice of drug to lower blood pressure. Through the 1990s, there was a group of clinicians who were concerned that the calcium channel blocking drugs (CCBDs) family of antihypertensive were detrimental. These concerns were effectively addressed by studies using amlodipine, nitrendipine and nifedipine. The predicted outcomes were achieved, based on blood pressure reduction, with no unexplained adverse effects. Newer drugs including angiotensin converting enzyme inhibitors (ACEIs) and angiotensin receptor blockers (ARBs) gave results that also were predictable on the blood pressure reduction. It seemed that the primary driver for the reduction in event rate and improvement in the pathology of hypertension was the reduction in blood pressure itself, rather than the specific agents involved. The original British Hypertension Society algorithm for medication, which had concentrated on β-blocker-thiazide combinations as per the original trials, was modified to include these newer agents.

Then came the Anglo-Scottish Cardiovascular Outcomes Trial (ASCOT), which compared a traditional β-blocker-thiazide combination with a CCBD-ACEI combination. Failure to control with one set of drugs involved cascade to an α-blocker and centrally acting agents, not to drugs from the other arm. The results were startling, as the trial was stopped early because of an excess of events in the β-blocker-thiazide arm. There was a small difference in blood pressure favouring the newer drugs, but this was insufficient to explain the event rate difference. In addition, there was a significant reduction in the development of new-onset diabetes in the CCBD-ACEI arm. Paradoxically, the decision to stop the trial early (taken independently by the data and safety monitoring board) meant that some of the other statistically important parameters could not be checked. ASCOT has been widely interpreted as showing that the β-blocker-thiazide combination is detrimental to diabetic risk, and has resulted in the modified algorithm for antihypertensive therapy relegating β-blockade to a distant fourth in the drug selection cascade.

Accepting this proviso on β-blockers, the past 50 years have seen consistent trial evidence on the use of blood pressure lowering drugs, their safety and efficacy and their applicability to large numbers of individuals with raised blood pressure. The level of intervention does not depend upon the drugs themselves, but upon our willingness to support this intervention in a substantial proportion of the population who are currently asymptomatic.

Key points

- There is a clear relationship between high blood pressure, increased cardiovascular risk, and event rate.
- Large trials, and trials in subgroups, have confirmed the benefit in treating blood pressure, producing a reduction in cardiovascular events, with no J-shaped curve for adverse events with lower blood pressure values.
- With the exception of β-blockers, there is little to choose between different antihypertensives (though specific drug approaches may be chosen for different patient groups).
- Since blood pressure increases with age in westernised adults, the decision on treatment levels for mild to moderate hypertension is influenced by society and pharmaco-economics.

Further reading

Dahlof B, Sever PS, Poulter NR et al. (2005) Prevention of cardiovascular events with an antihypertensive regimen of amlodipine adding perindopril as required versus atenolol adding bendroflumethiazide as required, in the Anglo-Scandinavian Outcomes Trial - Blood Pressure Lowering Arm (ASCOT-BPLA): a multicentre randomised controlled trial. Lancet 366(9489), 895–906.

Lewington S, Clarke R, Qizilbash N, Peto R, Collins R. (2002) Prospective Studies Collaboration. Age-specific relevance of usual blood pressure to vascular mortality: a meta-analysis of individual data for one million adults in 61 prospective studies. Lancet 360(9349), 1903–1913.

Stamler J, Wentworth D, Neaton JD. (1986) Is relationship between serum cholesterol and risk of premature death from coronary heart disease continuous and graded? Findings in 356 222 primary screenees of the Multiple Risk Factor Intervention Trial (MRFIT). JAMA 256, 2823–2828.

3   CARDIOVASCULAR RISK

The concept of cardiovascular risk is central to an appreciation of trials, guidelines and targets. But as humans we are poor at judging risk, especially technological risk. People will avoid aeroplanes but drive a lot, will purchase lottery tickets but worry about asteroid strikes. So risks are usually expressed in digestible, 10-year bites.

The major difficulty is in understanding absolute and relative risk. Absolute risk is finite, often also named total risk. If 100 people had the same risk factors, how many events would there be over the next 10 years? Relative risk is a comparison with individuals who do not have the same risk cluster. If the patient is compared to an age- and sex-matched individual without risk, how many more times are they likely to have an event? So absolute or total risk may be represented as 10%, 20%, etc. Relative risk may be twofold, fivefold, etc. A young, fit man with a high blood pressure may have a low absolute risk, but a high relative risk, compared to his risk with a normal blood pressure. An elderly fit woman with a high blood pressure may have a high absolute risk, as pathologies become more common with age, but not have an especially high relative risk, if all her other risk factors are low.

These risks apply very well to groups as they are statistically derived. People often wish to know their own, defined, medical risk. This is of course impossible to compute, depending as it does on many factors, societal as well as medical. Jumping out of an aircraft is risky. Parachute failure is regarded as fatal, but has a defined survivability – it is just very small. Hugh Tunstall-Pedoe's risk disc expressed risk in relative but readily understandable terms. Imagine a queue of 100 people of the same sex and age, all waiting for a heart attack – what is the individual's position in this queue? Although the risk disc isn't used commonly, this concept remains useful in discussion with those considering risk-altering changes, lifestyle as well as drugs.

Population risk is a more reliable statistic. Any change in the population mean for an identifiable risk factor will have a predictable health effect. Reducing the mean alcohol consumption per head will reduce alcohol-based liver disease in an expected manner. This is a good example, as there is a bell-shaped curve for alcohol consumption, just as for blood pressure and cholesterol values. Indeed, the reduction in mean cholesterol in the Finnish population has produced the predicted fall in cardiovascular events. Like alcohol, there is overlap between the mean values for individuals affected by pathology and those who are not. There are two consequences from this. First, there will be a sizable cohort of individuals who are not obviously at high cardiovascular risk, but who will proceed to a cardiovascular event; they may not be readily identifiable before they have a clinical event. Second, lowering population mean blood pressure will reduce events largely by lowering risk in these individuals who are around the mean value. There are far more individuals in this group than at the upper end of the blood pressure distribution curve. Population strategies are therefore essential, as only in this way will these individuals be 'treated' before pathology strikes.

Given this, is it still worth screening? I would support the guideline view that it is. The incidence and prevalence of cardiovascular disease in our populations, and the fact that cost-effective treatments are available, should make screening a high priority for our society. Public health measures can only be reinforced by screening and individual knowledge. In addition, there are still sufficient asymptomatic individuals at the upper end of the risk distribution to make this worthwhile. Despite advances in therapy, more than 20% of first presentations with myocardial infarction are fatal. Finding and treating high-risk individuals remains a health-care goal.

The other concept of note is numbers needed to treat. Classically this is expressed as the number of patients in a given risk range who need to be treated with a specific intervention over a 5-year period in order to save one event.

Clearly, this has implications for treatment strategies. If resource for primary prevention is targeted at high absolute risk alone, a lot of elderly patients will get aggressive risk factor management. This doesn't do much for population risk, or added life year calculations. On the other hand, targeting younger individuals with high relative risk gives rise to very large numbers needed to treat in order to save one event.

With no easy answer to this paradox, the pragmatic approach of the current guidelines is to project the total risk of younger individuals to age 49, and to recommend treatment if this projected risk is high.

The other point to be noted in the newer guidelines is their reference to cardiovascular disease (CVD) risk, rather than coronary heart disease (CHD) risk. This therefore includes stroke risk (including transient ischaemic attack, TIA). A 10-year CHD risk of 15% is equivalent to a 10-year CVD risk of 20%, and this is the cut-point chosen for primary intervention.

How are these risks calculated? The largest single long-term database for cardiovascular risk comes from the Framingham study, and a series of equations has been constructed to calculate individual risk based on this population. Framingham is a small town outside Boston, chosen for study because of its size and its proximity. It was and still is far from ethnically diverse, and has a limited range of deprivation category scores. The Framingham equations are accurate for Caucasian, principally Anglo-Saxon males of low-moderate to high-moderate incomes – anything else is extrapolation. In the absence of better options, these equations have been the cornerstone of risk calculation for the past two decades. More recent and laudable attempts to adjust for ethnic origin and deprivation category have some early validation, but are not fully refined. So, for example, the Framingham offspring data (as opposed to the original equations) omit predictions of cerebrovascular disease. The SCORE (Systematic Coronary Risk Evaluation) project data used in European tables contains European epidemiological data and predicts cardiovascular risk rather than just coronary risk, but is based on mortality figures, and so underestimates event rates and thereby total risk by omitting non-fatal events.

The Joint British Societies' Guidelines on Prevention of Cardiovascular Disease in Clinical Practice (JBS1) were originally published in 1998. These guidelines represented a unified approach to atherothrombotic disease prevention and management, with input from cardiology, diabetes, hypertension and lipid speciality organisations. Common protocols and a multifactorial approach to risk management were initiated. Since 1998 there have been considerable advances in evidence for hypertension and lipid management, both in high-risk individuals and in diabetes, and prophylaxis for the development of both diabetes and atherothrombosis. New Joint British Societies' Guidelines – JBS2 – were assembled with additional input from primary care and stroke physicians, and published in December 2005. This is a landmark document that is essential reading for all involved in the clinical management of cardiovascular risk.

The risk thresholds for intervention have altered between JBS1 and JBS2. The former were pragmatic and aimed at consensus and achievable targets. The newer guidelines build upon the consensus, are based upon global risk, and use newer data to aim for lower targets for individual risk factors. The priority groups for intervention are shown in Box 3.1. Essentially the risk threshold is of greater than 15% CHD risk, or 20% CVD risk, over a 10-year period. Of equal importance are the groups in Box 3.2. These are individuals with a 'lighthouse' risk, a single risk factor that is sufficiently elevated so as to invalidate any potential risk calculation. They are at sufficient risk as to require therapy regardless of any formal calculation.

Box 3.1   Priorities for CVD prevention in clinical practice

The following have equal priority in CVD risk management:

- individuals with any form of established atherosclerotic CVD
- individuals with diabetes mellitus (type 1 or 2)
- individuals with no symptoms and no overt CVD, but with a combination of risk factors that gives them an estimated 10-year CVD risk of >20%

Box 3.2   Single risk factors constituting lighthouse risk, requiring management regardless of apparent risk calculation

- individuals with elevated BP, >160 systolic or >100 diastolic, or with lower levels but evidence of target organ damage
- individuals with a total to HDL cholesterol ratio of >6
- individuals with familial dyslipidaemia, such as familial hypercholesterolaemia and familial combined hyperlipidaemia

---

The Guidelines also advocate a common sense clinical approach when faced with individuals who are likely to be at higher risk, even though this cannot be formally calculated. Examples include those with obesity, a

Table 3.1 Protocol for assessment of hypertension*

BP >160 and/or >100	Treat
BP 140–159 and/or 90–99	Assess global risk
Total risk ≥20%; or target organ damage; or diabetes	Lifestyle advice; monitor BP; treat <140/85 for risk ≥20%; <130/80 for diabetes; target organ damage
Total risk <20%; no organ damage; no diabetes	Lifestyle advice; monitor BP; reassess CVD risk yearly

*Measure BP as part of total CVD risk assessment.

strong family history of premature CVD, women with early menopause, and lipid risk from low HDL or raised triglycerides. They also point out the ethnic basis for the risk calculation, and advise caution if extrapolating; ethnic Asians in particular will have their risk underestimated by these charts. Finally, the Guidelines propose using risk from untreated values if recalculating risk – say, for example, in adopting high-risk targets. A patient may have a blood pressure of 125/70 mmHg on therapy, but if the value was 155/95 mmHg before treatment, then this value should be used for any further calculations. Similarly, lifetime cigarette exposure may be more important than current consumption. The emphasis throughout is on a pragmatic approach to risk, and to err on the side of over- rather than under-estimating this risk.

In the UK the General Medical Services contract in primary care has selected targets and audit standards for risk factor management. This represents the biggest single public health initiative in the field of cardio-vascular disease since food rationing after 1945. It is, however, an appropriate response to a growing epidemic.

Key points

- Absolute (total) risk is the finite risk of an event for an individual over a finite time span.
- Relative risk is the risk of an event for an individual, compared to the same individual's risk if a risk factor has been modified or removed.

- Relative risk is constant across age ranges; in age-related pathologies such as cardiovascular disease, absolute risk will rise with age.
- Population screening will identify asymptomatic individuals at high relative risk.
- A decision to treat such individuals may be graded by their absolute risk, based on cost-effectiveness.
- Population strategies to lower mean risk parameters will reach individuals who are not at apparent high risk, but who nonetheless comprise the bulk of those who proceed to a cardiovascular event.
- Risk calculations are still based on the original Framingham equations; these aren't perfect, particularly in some ethnic groups, but they are the best available for the present.
- There are individuals with 'lighthouse' risk, a single risk factor sufficiently high so as to invalidate risk calculations.
- The new Joint British Societies' Guidelines form a template for screening and treating cardiovascular risk, with targets for risk profiles for normal and for high-risk groups.
- The General Medical Services contract contains risk targets which are an appropriate start point for our medical response to the epidemic of cardiovascular disease.

References and further reading

British Cardiac Society, British Hypertension Society, Diabetes UK, HEART UK, Primary Care Cardiovascular Society, The Stroke Association (Wood D *et al.*) (2005) JBS2: Joint British Societies' guidelines on prevention of cardiovascular disease in clinical practice. *Heart* **91**(Suppl V), v1–v52.

Scottish Intercollegiate Guidelines Network (SIGN) (2007) Risk estimation and the prevention of cardiovascular disease – a national clinical guideline. Edinburgh: SIGN.

4 PATHOPHYSIOLOGY OF HYPERTENSION

Hypertension is a multifactorial disease, and this is not a pathology textbook. However, it is important to understand some of the mechanisms producing raised blood pressure, in terms of looking at end-organ damage from the process, investigation of various possible pathologies, and the mechanisms of drug action. What follows therefore is a walk through some of the more important pathophysiology of hypertension. Detailed pathology texts are advised for the more enquiring.

Physiology

Blood pressure is a function of cardiac output and peripheral resistance – the amount of blood being pumped, and the back pressure against the pump action. The simple physics of this is only rarely affected by cardiac output as such, which is relatively stable except during exercise. The peripheral resistance is provided by the arterial tree, and the bulk of this comes from the small vessels at arteriolar level. Blood pressure is thus largely controlled by arteriolar tone, the amount of constriction in the smooth muscle cells in the blood vessel wall.

In Western (wo)man, arteriolar tone increases with age, as does blood pressure. This seems to be part of normal senescence, except that it does not occur in more primitive societies, especially those with a low salt intake. Further, migrating peoples will demonstrate blood pressure rises and this apparent senescence process as they adopt a more westernised diet, or at least a higher salt intake. The genetics of hypertension and of salt handling are under intense investigation. This is not to suggest that salt intake is the only factor, but it is a useful starting point.

Other factors control smooth muscle vascular tone, as shown in Table 4.1. This immediately gives the logic behind the mechanisms of action of some antihypertensives. For example, calcium channel blocking drugs

Table 4.1 Factors controlling smooth muscle arteriolar tone

Local	Smooth muscle	Autonomic nerves
		Auto regulation
		Intracellular calcium
	Endothelial	Nitric oxide
		Endothelin
	Hormonal	Renin–angiotensin
		Kallkrein-bradykinin
		Catecholamines
		Prostaglandins
		Thromboxanes
Circulating		Renin–angiotensin
		Catecholamines
		Atrial natriuretic peptide (ANP)

(CCBDs) alter the flux of the calcium ions required to enable contraction of the myofibrils within the smooth muscle cells, and so cause vasodilatation.

The autonomic nervous system has its major effect by direct innervation of the vasculature, with only small amounts of local catecholamines escaping from the neuromuscular end-plate junctions, and smaller amounts still in general circulation. However, this does play an important part in controlling peripheral resistance. Both α-blockers and β-blockers will lower blood pressure, and will do so in normotensives. Nitric oxide is a powerful vasodilator, and endothelin a powerful vasoconstrictor. They seem to be in local balance, affected by tissue damage and hypoxia. They are not therapeutic targets as yet, but it is worth noting that atherosclerotic lesions reduce the ability of the endothelium to synthesise nitric oxide, and of the underlying smooth muscle to respond (vasodilate) under its influence. In experimental models such as forearm dilatation in man, statins can restore the vasodilatory properties of the endothelium.

The renin–angiotensin–aldosterone system (RAAS) is at the centre of vasoconstriction mechanisms and of the therapeutic efforts to lower blood pressure. A little more detailed study of this mechanism is therefore required. Renin is an enzyme secreted by the juxtaglomerular apparatus (JGA) cells in the kidney. Its synthesis and release is increased by renal hypoperfusion. In circulation it acts upon angiotensinogen, a protein synthesised in the liver. This produces angiotensin I (ATI), which is in turn converted by angiotensin converting enzyme (ACE) to angiotensin II (ATII). This in turn binds to angiotensin receptors in kidney, brain, adrenal glands and vascular smooth muscle. By direct action, ATII is one of the most potent vasoconstrictors known. In addition, its brain action is to stimulate the sympathetic nervous system. Both by stimulating aldosterone production from the adrenals, and by direct effect on the kidney, it causes sodium retention. In short, when considering hypertension, this central role leads to the conclusion that the RAAS is one of the main villains of the piece. However, this neat physiological trail is false. Patients with hypertension often have no more activation of the RAAS than normotensives. The exceptions are those with renal and renovascular disease.

Nonetheless, there are several different therapeutic possibilities based upon the RAAS. β-Blockers block renin release, and also block the sympathetic drive from ATII. Drugs to directly antagonise the action of renin are under development; the first should be launched towards the end of 2007. Angiotensin converting enzyme inhibitors (ACEIs) block the production of ATII (except that they don't – see below). Angiotensin receptor blockers (ARBs) block the action of ATII in various tissues. Spironolactone is an aldosterone antagonist, and acts as a natriuretic (sodium excreting) diuretic. Finally, thiazide diuretics also act as natriuretics, and probably produce part of their hypotensive effect by modest volume depletion (though they also have a modest vasodilating effect). This natriuresis is offset by upregulation of the RAAS; combining an RAAS blocking drug with a thiazide diuretic thus potentiates the action of both compounds.

There is an important phenomenon known as 'ACEI escape'. This occurs because other natural kinin-like enzymes, particularly tissue plasminogen activator (tPA), are capable of over-converting ATI to ATII. To some extent these will upregulate when ACE is blocked. In some patients this can occur to the extent that the effect of the ACEI is attenuated. The problem usually presents as escape of blood pressure control, and can be treated by co-administration of an ACEI and an ARB (or spironolactone). Note that the ACEI is not discontinued here, as this class of drugs has direct vascular properties that the ARBs do not.

In terms of the arteriolar picture, prolonged hypertension causes hypertrophy and hyperplasia of the smooth muscle cells. Eventually these can outgrow their intrinsic blood supply, and fibrinoid necrosis ensues. This has a classical appearance on biopsy, particularly in renal tissue. There is usually no limitation to flow until the lumen is more than 75% narrowed, a property of the physics of flow through pipes and tubes. Hence the clinical effects of hypertension can be completely silent until a threshold is reached. The narrowing process can be exacerbated by the pathology of atherothrombosis, just as hypertension causes endothelial damage and worsens atherothrombosis itself.

Lastly, hypertension seems to produce a low-grade hypercoagulability. In part this is from chronic endothelial damage and dysfunction, with activated platelets and low-grade thrombosis from raised prothrombotic factors, and in part from blood flow factors. These effects are quite subtle, but it explains the clinical mechanism and success of antiplatelet therapy in hypertensive patients.

Hypertensive damage

Hypertension causes widespread damage throughout the vascular tree, either of itself or in combination with the atherothrombosis picture, starting with smaller blood vessels and progressing to large vessel damage. The potential is present to cause or exacerbate pathology in any vascular bed. In terms of end-organ damage, heart, brain, eyes and kidneys are the usual targets that produce significant clinical manifestations.

Heart

The main manifestation of hypertension in the heart is of left ventricular hypertrophy (LVH). In part this muscular hypertrophy is due to the continuous stroke work of pumping against a high peripheral vascular resistance. Circulating factors, particularly the RAAS factors, may also contribute, which possibly explains the efficacy of ACEIs in regressing LVH. A patient with LVH has a fourfold risk of a cardiac event compared to an isotensive patent without LVH. The thickened heart muscle outgrows its own blood supply, leading to angina, cardiac rhythm problems and ischaemic events, and insidious cardiac failure. Hypertension is also a powerful risk for conventional atherothrombosis, worsening the risk of coronary heart disease. 'Hypertensive cardiomyopathy' is really ischaemic cardiomyopathy in the hypertrophied, hypertensive heart.

Brain

The commonest manifestation of hypertension in the brain is of an atherothrombotic infarct arising from an intracranial blood vessel. Hypertension is also a risk for pure intracerebral haemorrhage, for sub-arachnoid haemorrhage, and for small vessel brain ischaemia. The last of these may not be obvious except on MRI scanning, and may explain the association between hypertension and cognitive impairment in the elderly.

Eyes

Fundoscopy allows direct visualisation of small blood vessels in the cerebral arterial tree. Background changes are relatively common, but haemorrhages, exudates and papilloedema denote an emergency. Acute visual problems are the province of the ophthalmologist.

Kidney

Hypertension can cause renal disease, and renal disease can cause hypertension. The classical small vessel fibrinoid necrosis causes hypertensive nephrosclerosis on biopsy, although at end stage this pathology is indistinct. Because this is a glomerular pathology, the first sign of damage is microalbuminuria, with or without trace haematuria. If this isn't looked for, it will be missed. Early and aggressive blood pressure control can halt renal decline and even reverse this. The ACEI/ARB group of drugs are particularly effective here, as there is often a high renin component to the hypertension. However, glomerular filtration pressure is dependent on the difference between afferent and efferent arteriolar tone at the glomerulus, and efferent tone is ATII dependent. Sometimes ACEIs will increase renal blood flow and reduce proteinuria but decrease glomerular filtration rate (GFR). This is particularly a problem in renal artery stenosis, where the hypertension is driven at least in part by an activated RAAS from the hypoperfused kidney; the glomeruli in this kidney are very dependent on ATII efferent tone to maintain any sort of filtration pressure in the face of the low delivered pressure behind the stenosis.

Causes of hypertension

It is conventional to describe hypertension as 'essential' or secondary. This deceptive nomenclature is used to conceal the fact that, in the patients with essential disease, we do not know what has caused the process. In patients with secondary hypertension, there is a defined, separate, responsible pathology. Across all ages, less than 5% of hypertensives have a secondary cause, though this is higher in younger patients. As described in the chapter on investigation, the pragmatic approach is to baseline investigate all hypertensives (principally for target organ damage), and look for secondary hypertension in younger patients, and in those in whom there is some clue from the history, clinical examination, or baseline tests. Further investigation can then be triggered if the patient is refractory to treatment. The more common potential secondary causes of hypertension are discussed here.

Renal disease

Intrinsic renal disease can cause hypertension by salt and water retention, and can be the first manifestation of a more generalised autoimmune disease or arthritis. Haematuria, proteinuria and impaired renal function should all be picked up during baseline screening. Other manifestations or the history may trigger an immunology screen.

Renovascular disease

Renal artery stenosis can cause hypertension as above. In mid-life and beyond this is usually due to atherothrombosis, and the patient may have other manifestations of this. In younger patients it is usually due to fibromuscular dysplasia (FMD). Atherothrombotic lesions are often ostial or just post-ostial, with a post-stenotic dilatation. FMD lesions have a typical beaded appearance.

Conn's syndrome

Overproduction of aldosterone by the adrenal glands produces hypertension, principally by salt and water retention. The cause is usually a solitary functioning adenoma, in which case surgical removal is indicated. Malignancies (of adrenal or elsewhere) are rare, but bilateral adrenal hyperplasia can be found. Apparently normal adrenals should be kept under review, as there is a small but definite incidence of subsequent adenoma, presumably lesions that have been below the detection threshold of the scanning modality.

Cushing's syndrome

Excess glucocorticoid has mineralocorticoid activity, and so Cushing's can produce direct hypertension, as well as by obesity. In fact it can be difficult to distinguish morbid obesity from Cushing's, especially if there is a significant alcohol history with the obesity. If a short dexamethasone suppression test does not do so, endocrine referral should be considered.

Phaeochromocytoma

Overproduction of catecholamines by the adrenal glands can be fairly constant or episodic. The former is confusing in terms of the lack of paroxysms in the history, but shows up readily in investigation. The latter gives a more classical history but can be missed on biochemical investigation. More than 90% of phaeochromocytomas are pathologically benign, although the hormone production can be anything but. Resection is then a cure. The difficulty is having the correct level of clinical suspicion.

Carcinoid syndrome

For a carcinoid tumour to release serotonin and related products into the systemic circulation, the tumour must be in either the lungs or the liver. Lung disease may be benign, but liver tumours almost always represent metastases from a gut primary. The liver can metabolise these products from the primary on first pass, and so gut tumours can go biochemically undetected. Paroxysmal flushing and diarrhoea are the hallmarks of the clinical presentation. Specialist endocrine medical and surgical management are required.

Other endocrine causes

Acromegaly, hyperparathyroidism, hyperthyroidism and sex hormone anomalies can present with hypertension. They are usually detected by history or by routine blood testing, though acromegaly can be difficult. Polycystic ovarian syndrome is particularly worth consideration, and responds to metformin (and weight loss).

Exogenous substances

Various ingested compounds can produce hypertension. Hormone replacement therapy (HRT) and the oral contraceptive pill (OCP) should be prescription-based, although the latter may have been obtained through a family planning service. Non-prescription drugs can raise blood pressure, especially cocaine, and anabolic steroids.

Key points

- Blood pressure is a function of cardiac output and peripheral resistance; in pathological hypertension it is usually the latter that is a problem.
- Blood pressure rises with age in Western societies though not in less developed cultures.
- The reasons for this are not clear, but salt intake and the genetics of sodium handling may provide some clues.
- Hypertension damages small blood vessels.
- Hypertension also combines with other risk factors to accelerate the process of atherosclerosis (or atherothrombosis).
- Hypertension causes insidious target organ damage, principally in brain, heart, kidneys and eyes.
- Clinical events present late on in this process, but target organ screening can detect damage earlier.
- Hypertension also causes a low-grade hypercoagulability state, which explains the additional effectiveness of aspirin in treating hypertensive risk.
- The renin–angiotensin–aldosterone system (RAAS) has a central role in maintaining blood pressure, and is an attractive target for therapeutic interventions.
- The term 'essential hypertension' is used to conceal the fact that the cause of raised blood pressure isn't understood in most cases.
- Secondary causes of hypertension are relatively rare, though more common in younger individuals.

Further reading

Carton J, Daly R, Ramani P. (2006) *Clinical Pathology*. Oxford: OUP.

5   METABOLIC SYNDROME AND DIABETES

As we enter the second half of this decade, it is clear that one of the major challenges for health-care providers in the developed world is a disease of plenty. The epidemic of obesity and subsequent glucose handling disorders brings in its wake an increase in cardiovascular risk and disease that will challenge our systems in the same way as epidemics of infectious diseases did in the first decade of the previous century. A generation of ill-health and high health service requirement is on its way, and most of this ill-health will manifest itself in cardiovascular outcomes. This chapter considers the specific problems associated with diabetes and the metabolic syndrome, with particular regard to hypertension risk. The other cardiovascular risks of these conditions – lipids, cardiomyopathy, etc. – are outside the remit of this short work, but aggressive treatment of all the associated cardiovascular risk factors is mandatory.

Definitions

There is a continuous spectrum of risk and of disease profile across the whole range of glucose handling disorders. The specifics of providing diagnostic criteria involve the imposition of cut-points on this spectrum. It is well worth remembering that the original definition of diabetes from the oral glucose tolerance test, as decided by the WHO more than 30 years ago, was based on an appreciation of which individuals would progress to microvascular complications, particularly retinopathy and nephropathy. A cut-point process based on macrovascular disease – heart attack and stroke – would have come to different conclusions. This has been recognised to some extent by a relaxation of the diagnostic criteria for diabetes from the American Diabetes Association to include a simple fasting glucose of ≥ 7 mmol/l. Impaired fasting glucose is a glucose of between 6.1 and 7 mmol/l.

The metabolic syndrome has more names than any other commonly occurring pathology. It is characterised by the quartet of central (visceral) obesity, hypertension, dyslipidaemia and insulin resistance. All these elements are progressive, and the insulin resistance is the key. As abdominal girth expands, individuals remain euglycaemic but with increasing insulin levels. As the resistance pattern becomes established, glucose handling becomes more formally disordered, passing through impaired fasting glucose to impaired glucose tolerance and finally to type 2 diabetes. Not all obese individuals develop the syndrome. Central, visceral obesity is required, and there may well be a genetic component to where excess adipose tissue builds up. In addition, younger women tend to deposit fat subcutaneously if overweight, only moving to a visceral pattern after the menopause.

There is no requirement for biochemical or metabolic testing to establish this syndrome. If an individual has a waist–hip ratio of greater than 1, then the diagnosis is made. More recently, an absolute waist circumference of more than 40 inches in a man, and 35 inches in a woman, have been proposed to establish the diagnosis. Note that there is a marked ethnic difference for Asians, who are more prone to the syndrome; the corresponding figures are 36 inches for a man and 31 inches in a woman.

Finally, in terms of type 1 and type 2 diabetes, although the pathogenic mechanisms are different, the atherosclerotic risk is the same. Now that type 1 patients routinely live more than 30 years after diagnosis, and avoid or survive their microvascular complications, it can be seen that they proceed to develop macrovascular disease, with a second phase morbidity and mortality from cardiovascular complications. Similarly, if aggressive management of cardiovascular risk enables type 2 patients to defy their macrovascular disease despite less than perfect glycaemic control, then these patients will develop the retinopathy and nephropathy of microvascular pathology.

Metabolic syndrome

The presence of metabolic syndrome confers of itself a considerable cardiovascular risk. Each of the specific parts of the quartet should be addressed.

Affected individuals are hypertensive, and this must be treated. Even before the ASCOT results, there was a strong drive towards treating the blood pressure with metabolically neutral drugs, and this is now mandatory. Under no circumstances should β-blockers be used in this condition, except for the treatment of angina; if this is required, care should be taken to avoid a concomitant thiazide diuretic. It is very difficult to lose weight whilst taking a β-blocker, and weight loss is a key management strategy. The ASCOT data emphasise the risk of precipitating diabetes in this group with poor drug selection. Instead, RAAS drugs and CCBDs form the cornerstone of the therapeutic approach. Given the clustering of risk in this condition, and the near diabetic levels of global risk, it is good practice to treat such patients to diabetic targets. This inevitably means polypharmacy for these patients.

The visceral obesity is difficult to treat, because it involves the adoption of a calorie-limited diet and an exercise profile. Getting middle-aged people to adopt and sustain such lifestyle changes is extremely difficult. Nonetheless, the data are clear. If a diet and exercise programme is successful, and the individual loses abdominal girth, many of the metabolic features revert towards normal. Well-motivated individuals who sustain these changes are often able to discontinue antihypertensive medication, and to reduce or stop lipid-lowering therapy. Sadly, in our clinical practice, such patients are in the minority. The chapter on lifestyle changes contains more detail on diet, exercise and drugs for weight loss.

The question of whether to treat the insulin resistance as such is difficult. Insulin-sensitising drugs include metformin, the thiazolidinediones, or glitazones, and the new DPP-4 drugs. The glitazones may not cause net weight loss, but do change the pattern of obesity from visceral to subcutaneous, which is of benefit. Metformin does cause net weight loss, and it is the visceral fat that is lost. DPP-4 drugs inhibit dipeptidyl peptidase-4, the enzyme that degrades glucagon-like peptide 1 (GLP1). Increasing the circulating levels of this natural balancing hormone for insulin boosts insulin sensitivity and can protect β-cell mass. The clinical trials of the DDP-4 drugs in diabetes are promising, but the hope is that they can arrest progression of metabolic syndrome. None of these classes of drug is licensed for obesity or for metabolic syndrome. However, an informed discussion with the patient can result in a therapeutic trial. In particular, the author has used metformin in prediabetic patients with a refractory lipid profile.

The lipid profile found in common in metabolic syndrome, prediabetes and frank diabetes is far more atherogenic than the specific parameters would suggest. The total cholesterol is mildly elevated, the high density lipoprotein (HDL) is low, and the triglycerides are also slightly raised. What this picture hides is that the HDL is mostly small and dense, which leads to its rapid catabolism and turnover, and that the low density lipoprotein (LDL) is also small and dense, and highly atherogenic of itself. The issue of whether or not the triglycerides are also of themselves atherogenic is moot; most therapeutic strategies will have some triglyceride effect. Aggressive management of this lipid profile in and of itself is an integral part of the global risk approach. Clinicians should commit patients to polypharmacy for the treatment of this profile as necessary.

Diabetes and cardiovascular risk

It is now widely accepted that diabetes poses an increased cardiovascular risk, largely through the effect of accelerated atherothrombosis. Impaired glucose tolerance is associated with an increased relative cardiovascular risk of 1.5- to twofold, and formal diabetes with an increase of two- to fourfold. This means that patients with formal diabetes have a risk profile very similar to patients who already have overt cardiovascular disease. Unfortunately, many patients without a diagnosis of diabetes at the time of a cardiovascular event will have the diagnosis made shortly afterwards; this is particularly true of myocardial infarction.

By a logical extension of this, newer guidelines have dispensed with separate risk tables for diabetic patients. Instead, anyone with diabetes is regarded as being at risk. The approach that has been adopted in the JBS2 guidelines is to treat all diabetics older than 40, both type 1 and type 2, as being at high risk and as such qualifying automatically for aggressive risk factor management. Younger diabetics will also qualify if they have overt cardiovascular disease already, or if they have one of a number of other factors either contributing to or as a marker of increased risk. These factors are shown in Box 5.1.

So most individuals with diabetes will be committed to aggressive risk factor modification, certainly at the age of 40 if not before, and irrespective of whether they have type 1 or type 2 diabetes. How to manage the blood pressure part of this risk? First, the lower targets in such patients will mandate polypharmacy. Second, the important message from the UK Prospective Diabetes Study (UKPDS) is of tighter blood pressure control; the study was not powered to distinguish between outcomes on ACEI versus β-blocker, given equal blood pressure. Third, there is an accumulating body of evidence in favour of RAAS drugs, not just in terms of renal outcome, but also for global CVD event rate. Lastly, good blood pressure control in diabetics also reduces the microvascular complications, not just nephropathy as above, but also retinopathy. The pragmatic approach adopted is to treat with RAAS drugs first line, and add CCBDs and diuretics thereafter. In effect, diabetics are regarded as if they are all under 55 in age, and commenced on an ACEI or ARB initially. As above, β-blockers are avoided unless there is angina. Note that many diabetics have autonomic dysfunction, and a postural drop. This is worth checking, as α-blockers may exacerbate it, and a centrally acting drug may be preferred.

Clearly the management of diabetic patients encompasses their entire cardiovascular risk profile, and just as for metabolic syndrome patients, lipid-lowering therapy, diet, exercise and weight optimisation are important. I would also emphasise the importance of good diabetic control. Triglycerides in particular are very responsive to the state of the background diabetes, rising sharply with rising HbA1c. In addition to any direct atherogenic potential they may have, raised triglycerides are a marker for the state of the LDL, with more small, dense LDL present as the triglycerides become higher. This small dense LDL is highly pathogenic itself, and prone to modification (oxidation, glycation, or both) to further enhance its potential atherogenicity. In short, there is little net gain to aggressive risk factor modification in diabetic patients unless the diabetes control itself comes under scrutiny. Good control is integral to risk factor management, and again we should be prepared to commit to polypharmacy to help achieve this. The most common consequence of this in clinical practice is the initiation or continuation of insulin-sensitising drugs – metformin, a glitazone – in type 2 diabetic patients who have been converted to insulin therapy. This is especially important in those individuals who have both type 2 diabetes and metabolic syndrome, and who are at considerable cardiovascular risk.

Key points

- There is a continuous spectrum of cardiovascular risk across all glucose handling disorders; all such patients are at some degree of enhanced risk.
- The metabolic syndrome conveys particular risk, both of itself and in combination with a formal diagnosis of diabetes.
- Metabolic syndrome consists of hypertension, dyslipidaemia, insulin resistance and central (visceral) obesity; it is readily diagnosed with a tape measure for abdominal girth.
- Diet, lifestyle, exercise and weight optimisation are key in the management of these disorders, though insulin-sensitising drugs are an important adjunct.
- The analyses for cardiovascular risk do not distinguish between type 1 and type 2 diabetes – all are at high risk.
- All diabetics over the age of 40 merit aggressive risk factor management.
- Diabetics aged under 40 but with additional risk factors also merit aggressive risk factor management.
- The blood pressure risk is exacerbated by the glucose handling disorder, and more aggressive blood pressure targets are adopted.

- The blood pressure risk profile in diabetics and metabolic syndrome patients will require more than one antihypertensive agent.
- Metabolically neutral antihypertensives are mandatory, with RAAS drugs (ACEIs and ARBs) and CCBDs as first-line options.
- There is additional evidence in favour of RAAS drugs favourably affecting renal outcome.
- There is evidence of worse outcome in patients treated with β-blocker-thiazide combination; the β-blocker is thought to be the culprit, and should be avoided unless there is angina.
- Diabetics may have autonomic dysfunction and a postural drop; this should be checked, especially if an α-blocker is considered.
- The lipid risk is contained within the atherogenic lipid profile, consisting of slightly elevated total cholesterol, low HDL, and modestly elevated triglycerides; because of the modifications of the lipoprotein subfractions this profile is much more pathogenic than it appears in standard analysis.
- Statins are the first-line therapy for lipid risk, except in those cases where the triglyceride levels threaten pancreatitis, when a fibrate should be used initially.
- The lipid risk profile in diabetic and metabolic syndrome patients will often require more than one lipid-modifying drug.
- The lipid risk profile will be refractory to treatment if good diabetic control is neglected.

Further reading

Arauz-Pacheco C, Parrott MA, Raskin P; American Diabetes Association (2004) Hypertension management in adults with diabetes. *Diabetes Care* **27,** S65–S67.

Kahn R, Buse J, Ferrannini E, Stern M. (2005) The metabolic syndrome: time for a critical appraisal: joint statement from the American Diabetes Association and the European Association for the Study of Diabetes. *Diabetes Care* **28,** 2289–2304. (A controversial appraisal which sparked a lot of debate but contains a lot of useful background)

Metabolic syndrome. Finnish Medical Society Duodecim. Guidelines. Available at www.guideline.gov

6   INVESTIGATION OF HYPERTENSION

There are four sections to this chapter, namely, investigation for hypertension – the measurement of blood pressure; investigation for the effects of hypertension – screening for end-organ damage; investigation for the causes of hypertension; and parallel investigation of other risk factors.

Measurement of blood pressure

Despite the critical nature of this relatively straightforward procedure, it is still performed badly in routine practice. The essential features are outlined in the JBS2 Guidelines and repeated here.

- Use a properly maintained, calibrated and validated device.
- Measure sitting blood pressure.
- Measure standing blood pressure as well in the elderly and in diabetics.
- Remove tight clothing, support the arm at heart level, ensure that the arm is relaxed, and don't talk during the measurement.
- Use a cuff of the appropriate size.
- Lower the pressure by 2 mm/s, i.e. relatively slowly.
- Read the blood pressure to the nearest 2 mm.
- Measure the diastolic as the disappearance of sounds (Korotkov V).
- Take the mean of at least two readings, or more if there is a marked disparity.
- Do not treat on the basis of an individual reading.

To this I would add the following:

- Measure the BP in both arms at least once in patients with overt cardiovascular disease (in case of subclavian atherosclerosis).
- Perform lying and standing BP readings if there is doubt over a postural drop.

- If there is no Korotkov V (disappearance of sound), then Korotkov IV (diminution of sound) can be used but must be documented.
- Electronic devices are generally accurate but can misfire in patients with valvular heart disease and/or atrial fibrillation, and in those with incompressible vessels.
- Repeated measurements tend to bottom out after four measurements.
- White coat effect can only be reliably diagnosed by ambulatory blood pressure monitoring (ABPM).

Many patients now ask about purchase of their own blood pressure monitors. The patient website of the British Hypertension Society provides up-to-date reviews of devices. Wrist monitors should be avoided. Monitors with average trackers can be invalidated by casual use by a third party; a simple non-averaging monitor and a diary is more reliable.

Ambulatory blood pressure monitoring is increasingly used both to tease out white coat effect (in both normotensives and hypertensives), and to look for the absence of a nocturnal dip, an important prognosticator of progression and other pathologies. The commonly available machines are reliable and simple to use. The usual settings are to inflate every 15 minutes during the day, and every 30 minutes overnight, namely from 22:00 to 07:00. Many patients are intolerant of the overnight readings, but this should always be attempted. Loss of a nocturnal dip is an important finding. Surprisingly labile BP readings may be obtained in some patients, but a true white coat effect is confined to the first hour or so of the trace. ABPMs are particularly helpful in the anxious, the pregnant and the elderly. It is mandatory to check a manual BP in both arms before placing the device (and to use the higher reading arm in case of discrepancy). Finally, ABPMs read 10/5 or so **lower** than a casual or office reading, and the reporting thresholds of the device **must** be set accordingly. Thus an individual with an 'office' BP target of 140/90 will have an ABPM target of 130/85.

Investigation for the effects of hypertension

Screening for end-organ damage is a rapid and efficient means of stratifying the risk more accurately for individual patients, and targeting more aggressive therapy where needed. A good clinical history is part of this process, including family history. Assuming the absence of a previous event, then the main target organs are eyes, heart and kidneys.

Fundoscopy is straightforward and in most cases can be achieved in a darkened room, without the need for mydriatics. Hypertensive retinopathy is graded 0–4, but in most cases it is better to simply describe and record the findings. Silver wiring, vessel tortuosity and arteriovenous nipping are all more common with increasing age, even in normotensives, and are of less value in the elderly. Smaller retinal infarcts (dots and cotton-wool spots) are more concerning. Flame haemorrhages and papilloedema constitute an emergency regardless of age.

Clinical cardiomegaly is difficult to establish unless marked, especially in the obese or those with chronic obstructive pulmonary disease (COPD). An ECG is mandatory in all 'first-time' hypertensives. It may reveal unsuspected ischemic damage or conduction anomalies, but the main purpose is to assess LVH. Unfortunately the ECG is not reliable in this regard. In an effort to avoid deluging the echocardiography service with all hypertensives, the pragmatic approach is to reserve echo for those under 55 with ECG voltage hypertrophy, and for those in whom there is either a disparity between clinical and ECG findings, or some other clinical indication for scanning.

Renal damage from hypertension is almost always accompanied by some degree of albuminuria. A morning urine specimen should be brought by the patient, and tested for standard proteinuria and haematuria (and glycosuria) using a multistix or equivalent. If these are negative, then a test for microalbumin can be performed on the same sample, either using a specific microalbumin stick, or by sending to the Biochemistry Laboratory. Microalbuminuria is an early marker of renal damage in hypertension as well as diabetes, and a predictor for those requiring more aggressive therapy.

As part of the routine work-up for hypertension, bloods will also be drawn for other risk factors (e.g. lipids). In terms of end-organ damage, all patients will have urea and electrolytes drawn, including creatinine and (in most laboratories) an eGFR.

Investigation for the causes of hypertension

Most hypertensive patients do not have an identifiable medical cause for their hypertension, as outlined earlier. Submitting all comers to a full battery of exhaustive and invasive tests is inappropriate and potentially dangerous. The old days of an intravenous urogram (IVU) for everyone are long gone. But there will be some patients who have significant pathology, and the question is how to separate them from the majority who do not. What follows is pragmatic rather than evidence-based, but has served well in a clinical setting. It uses the concept of level testing, namely, to test to a certain level of probability or invasiveness, and then stop to assess response to medication, only moving to the next level if the clinical response is unsatisfactory.

Of the identifiable pathologies responsible for hypertension, the main four groups are:

- renal
- renovascular
- endocrine
- neuro-endocrine.

The level testing approach therefore is to exclude these where possible and/or clinically indicated.

Renal investigation starts with the family history and clinical examination. The presence of proteinuria and/or haematuria, or the finding of renal impairment on blood testing, generates further tests. These must include renal imaging (ultrasound is usually sufficient), quantification of proteinuria, and a renal immunology screen if there is haematuria. Remember also that haematuria may represent a second, unrelated pathology, and must never be ignored. Renal disease can cause hypertension, and hypertension can cause renal disease. Referral to urology or nephrology may be appropriate, depending upon the clinical setting.

Renovascular disease is usually atherothrombotic in older patients, and due to fibromuscular dysplasia (FMD) in the younger, especially females. The patient may give an arteriopathic history. Clinical examination may reveal diminished or absent foot pulses; 30–50% of such patients who are hypertensive will have some degree of renal artery stenosis. Or the patient may have had a deterioration in their renal function when started on a drug affecting the RAAS. Non-invasive assessment for renal artery stenosis is now available in three modalities – Doppler ultrasound, isotope renography, and magnetic resonance angiography. If indicated and

Box 6.1   Baseline consultation for the new hypertensive

Careful history, including:
- family history
- diet
- lifestyle

Clinical examination, to include:
- BP measurements as per the guidelines
- cardiovascular examination
- foot pulses
- fundoscopy
- search for bruits
- lipid stigmata (arcus, tendon xanthomata)

Urinalysis (including microalbuminuria)

ECG

Blood tests
- Biochemistry
  U/Es, eGFR
  LFTs, GGT
  Calcium, urate
  CK, TSH
  Glucose
  Cholesterol, HDL, triglycerides
- Haematology
  FBC
  PV

CK, Creatine kinase; ECG, electrocardiogram; eGFR, estimated glomerular filtration rate; FBC, full blood count; GGT, gamma-glutamyltransferase; HDL, high density lipoprotein; LFT, liver function test; PV, plasma viscosity; TSH, thyroid-stimulating hormone; U/Es, urea and electrolytes.

anatomically possible, formal renal angiography and angioplasty is usually technically successful. In FMD, angioplasty may return the BP to normal. In atherothrombotic disease, it usually does not, though it can reduce the tablet count. It will also protect against further or future renal deterioration, and against flash pulmonary oedema.

Endocrine investigation may not be necessary if the history reveals exogenous hormone – corticosteroids, HRT, OCP, or anabolic steroids. Cushing's syndrome can be hard to distinguish from severe obesity, both clinically and biochemically, but either a short or a long dexamethasone suppression test is usually sufficient; the former is easily performed in a primary care setting. Both obesity and Cushing's can also produce diabetes. Conn's syndrome is often accompanied by a low potassium (in the absence of a diuretic), and a high or high-normal sodium. It is usually refractory, except to spironolactone, and is often diagnosed by the combination of these features. Polycystic ovarian syndrome has a raised testosterone and a typical ultrasound appearance, and the clinical presentation includes menstrual difficulties and skin problems. Bodybuilders can be surprisingly reluctant to admit to anabolic use, but active users have a characteristically low HDL (<0.5).

Neuro-endocrine disease encompasses phaeochromocytoma and carcinoid tumours. If the latter, then it represents lung disease, or liver secondaries from a gastrointestinal primary. Flushing is a common presentation. Phaeochromocytomas are much more difficult to pin down, with very variable symptoms, or none. The ABPM may show wide fluctuations in pressure. The screening test for both of these is to perform three separate 24-hour urine collections. Most laboratories can now test for both catecholamines (for phaeochromocytoma) and 5-hydroxyindolacetic acid (5HIAA) (for carcinoid) on the same sample, and should provide instructions and a fact sheet for interfering substances to be avoided (such as vanilla, including ice-cream). Most of the phaeochromocytomas picked up in our clinic are on the basis of blind testing of young patients or refractory hypertension.

In summary, secondary causes of hypertension are considered when there is clinical index of suspicion, or clues from the family or personal history, or blood, urine or examination markers of some other disease process. Refractory hypertension (see Chapter 10), variable hypertension, and moderate to severe hypertension in the young are other factors.

Parallel investigation of other risk factors

Anyone with hypertension should have their global risk assessed. This assessment may trigger antihypertensive therapy where an isolated blood pressure picture may not. As above, a careful personal and family history are required. The other main risk factors are lipid profile, smoking and diabetes. Since any abnormality raises the prospect of therapy, it is often easier to measure the entire blood panel at the outset. This should therefore include a full blood count, a test for inflammation (CRP, PV), and biochemistry for U/Es (including creatinine and eGFR), LFTs and GGT, bone group, CK, TSH and urate. A glucose and lipid profile (Chol, HDL, Trig) accompanies this. If non-fasting triglycerides and glucose are normal, then they do not need to be repeated; if abnormal, a fasting sample repeat is required.

Key points

- Blood pressure is still poorly and inaccurately measured – see the text for recommendations.
- Do not treat on the basis of a single measurement.
- Electronic cuff devices are satisfactory in most patients; wrist monitors are less reliable.
- White coat effect can only be reliably diagnosed with ABPM.
- Note that ABPM reads at least 10/5 lower than office readings, and adjust accordingly.
- Target organ damage can stratify risk and must be performed – fundoscopy, urinalysis (including microalbumin) and ECG.
- Assessment of blood pressure should not occur in isolation – global cardiovascular risk must be assessed.
- Baseline investigations are shown above.
- Younger patients are more likely to have a cause for their hypertension, but the clinical yield of investigation is still low.
- Hypertensive arteriopaths often have renal artery stenosis.
- In the absence of clinical cues, in older patients the baseline investigations given are usually sufficient. More detailed investigations can be reserved for those who prove refractory to therapy.

Further reading

O'Brien E, Coats A, Owen P *et al.* (2000) Use and interpretation of ambulatory blood pressure monitoring: recommendations of the British Hypertension Society. *BMJ* **320,** 1128–1134.

7   DIET AND LIFESTYLE

The traditional diet and lifestyle approach to cardiovascular disease management has been overshadowed by the successes of the various drug therapies that are now available. However, this complete 'medicalisation' of risk is erroneous. There is still a considerable amount of risk that is amenable to straightforward advice, both for the population at large and for individuals at risk. An approach that incorporates lifestyle and non-drug modifications into a global risk management strategy is strongly advocated.

Smoking

A detailed analysis of smoking is not in the remit of this book. Suffice it to say that half of all smokers will die prematurely, from lung disease, cancer and atherothrombosis. Specifically for cardiovascular disease the risk calculation is clear, and smoking cessation is mandatory in any serious attempt to ameliorate this risk. Public health measures, including the bans on smoking in public places, are to be applauded, as there is a clear, defined risk from passive (or 'sidestream') smoking.

Patients who wish to stop smoking benefit from a combination of counselling and support measures, and pharmacological input. Hypnotherapy and acupuncture can be useful in certain individuals. Nicotine replacement therapy (NRT) is available as patches, chewing gum, sublingual tablets and inhalators, either on prescription or over the counter. Bupropion has recovered from some early adverse publicity to find a niche, though it is often reserved for those who fail NRT. Bupropion cannot be co-prescribed with antidepressants; the newer varenicline does not have this contraindication. There is no large trial showing that these pharmacological interventions cause a reduction in cardiovascular event rate, but this is a logical extrapolation from the smoking data already known.

Diet

Diet is a cornerstone of therapy. The safety, palatability and effectiveness of modern lipid-lowering therapy does not detract from the requirement for a basic low-fat, high-fibre, low-salt healthy eating diet. Patients are no longer required to 'earn' their drug therapy by trial of diet, but the role of diet in total risk management should be emphasised. Conversely, very restrictive diets are counterproductive; there are good data for long-term non-compliance with such diets, and drug therapy has made them unnecessary.

The role of the Mediterranean Diet has been explored both in primary and secondary settings, and the DASH diet has a proven efficacy. Conversely, there is surprisingly little data to back up the public health campaign for eating five servings of fresh fruit and vegetables per day. This is not to say that this is wrong, or should not be promoted, but that the evidence base is less robust. However, given that there is no harm profile from modifying the diet in this way, most authorities back this approach. Fish oil supplementation should be reserved for those who can't eat fish; far better to eat the real thing, preferably as a main course at least twice a week.

Finally, most individuals regard diet as pertaining to calories and weight. It is important to place this in context. Individuals may eat not very much but all the wrong things, and be slim but with hypertension and an adverse lipid profile. Or they can eat all the right things, but to excess, and be overweight or obese (with attendant risks) but with a relatively benign blood pressure and lipid profile – at least, until metabolic syndrome supervenes. Portion control is the key, and calorie intake should be balanced with exercise to optimise weight. Salt reduction is always beneficial, and individuals should be specifically counselled on the hidden salt and saturated fat (including hydrogenated fat) in ready-prepared, so-called 'value-added' meals. Rather than fad diets, an eating for life approach should be adopted. For individuals needing to lose weight, the Total Wellbeing Diet is useful, with a balanced intake, and includes sufficient protein to control satiety and appetite.

Salt

The modern, westernised diet of convenience and pre-processed foods contains a considerable excess of salt above that required for physiological maintenance. Salt is a habituator of our taste buds. We get used to it, and then food without it tastes bland. Reducing salt intake results in this bland taste for several weeks until the taste receptors reset. Salt reduction is thus a matter for education of the individual, and for public health and food industry initiatives. Estimates vary, but the average UK daily intake is thought to be about 9 g per day. Reducing this to 6 g per day would have the equivalent effect on blood pressure of taking a small dose of a single antihypertensive agent. Afro-Caribbeans and some older patients will be even more sensitive than this. Some patients replace sodium chloride with proprietary potassium chloride substitutes. These are effective in reducing salt intake. A diet rich in naturally occurring potassium (fruit and vegetables) also reduces blood pressure, but there are no grounds for recommending potassium supplementation *per se*. Note that potassium-containing substitutes must be used with caution in those with even mild renal impairment, and with potassium-conserving antihypertensives.

Obesity and exercise

Obesity and lack of exercise are inextricably linked. Whilst some people with low body mass index (BMI) do little exercise, and presumably have a high metabolic rate for other reasons, individuals with a high BMI or who are clinically obese almost invariably have a low exercise profile. There is little to be gained from an adversarial approach to this problem, and encouragement and advice should be offered.

Obesity results when calorie intake is greater the expenditure. It is important to note that this includes background metabolic rate as well as specific exercise expenditure. The value of an exercise programme in increasing basal metabolic rate should be emphasised. Portion control in a sensible balanced diet should be encouraged, and fad diets should be avoided. As above, the Total Wellbeing Diet is useful. For morbid obesity, a very low calorie diet may be required. This is the province of the specialist, usually hospital-based, with combined dietician and physician input.

Medications for obesity include orlistat, sibutramine and cannabinoid receptor antagonists. The first two include in their license indications that a weight loss programme should have commenced with some documented success before they are introduced. They are indicated for significant obesity, or for obesity in the presence of a significant co-morbidity or risk. This includes significant hypertension.

Orlistat acts by blocking pancreatic lipase. This reduces fat absorption from the gut. It is effective in combination with a reduction in calorie intake, and patients are advised to reduce their fat intake as a major part of this change. Compliance with the medication but not the diet produces unpleasant side-effects, principally steatorrhoea. Either by enforcing this diet change, or by direct action of the drug, orlistat can reduce the lipid profile, but is not licensed for this indication.

Sibutramine acts by suppressing appetite through its action on serotonin and noradrenaline re-uptake. This action is similar to that of antidepressants, which cannot therefore be co-prescribed. The drug is contraindicated by the presence of overt cardiovascular disease, which limits its usefulness somewhat, as does a propensity to cause or exacerbate hypertension.

Rimonibant is the first in a series of cannabinoid type 1 (CB1) receptor antagonists. These drugs have an effect on satiety, reducing appetite. They may also increase metabolic rate and decrease fat mass more directly, and are the subject of intensive research.

These drugs act in different ways and should be complimentary. However, a requirement for more than one of them should be a tripwire for onward referral to a specialist obesity service. Bariatric surgery is also the province of the specialist.

Exercise does not have to be particularly arduous in order to have an effect on metabolic rate. As little as 20–30 minutes of aerobic exercise is sufficient, three times a week. Patients can be guided by their maximum heart rate towards their aerobic effort range:

$$\text{Maximum heart rate} = 220 - \text{age}$$
$$\text{Aerobic range} = 60\text{--}80\% \text{ maximum heart rate}$$

Although all aerobic exercise is beneficial, non-weight-bearing exercise may be preferable for obese individuals, who should be encouraged to take up a range of exercises to minimise joint strain (and boredom). Swimming, cycling, rowing machines, exercise bikes and light weight workouts on cam (exercise) machines are all suitable. Some areas in the UK now have exercise on prescription, which should be explored. Like dietary changes, the intention is to achieve a fitness for life programme, rather than prowess in one particular area. Patients should be warned that converting fat to muscle will not reduce weight of itself, but is nonetheless beneficial, and that watching waist and clothing size may be as useful as total weight.

Alcohol

The relationship between alcohol and cardiovascular disease has been investigated very carefully over the last decade. There is a J-shaped (or 'hockey-stick') curve. Individuals with no alcohol intake have more cardiovascular disease than those who drink in moderation. Higher levels of alcohol intake are associated with an increasing mortality.

In part, this is due to the effect on the liver. Moderate alcohol increases HDL levels. Higher consumption begins to produce liver toxicity, with higher cholesterol and (in particular) triglycerides. With still higher consumption, or in sensitive individuals, there is both a hypertensive effect, and direct alcohol toxicity on the heart. As well as raising blood pressure directly, alcohol can raise blood pressure quite dramatically in periods of abstinence amongst those with a habitual high intake; such abstinence can often be triggered by upcoming clinic visits, for example. Interestingly, wine is indeed better than beer or spirits, with an additional anti-cancer as well as more cardiovascular protection. The Bandolier analysis for optimum alcohol consumption suggests that the most protection against 'all bad things', including heart attack, heart failure, stroke and cancer, is approximately half the Department of Health maximum, principally to be taken as wine. This works out as 14 units per week for a man, and 11 for a woman, with a regular daily intake of 1–2 units (rather than binges). Note that beer contains the most calories and salt, with brown beer worse than lager. Finally, despite extensive research at the University of Bordeaux, there are no large clinical trial data suggesting that red wine is better than white for cardiovascular protection.

Key points

- Smoking cessation is mandatory in any attempt to ameliorate cardiovascular risk.
- Diet and lifestyle advice have a major role to play in risk management.
- There is good evidence for a healthy eating, low-fat, high-fibre, reduced-salt diet, with additional fish intake.
- There is a large amount of salt hidden in the modern westernised diet, including in prepared and so-called 'value-added' foods, and in alcoholic drinks, particularly beer.
- Alcohol in moderation is beneficial, but in excess is harmful; current best estimates are for 14 units per week for men and 11 for women, as a regular intake. (Note that this is about half the current recommendations.)
- Regular exercise is beneficial.
- A diet and exercise programme to optimise weight is required in overweight individuals as an integral part of their risk management.

Further reading

Noakes M, Clifton P. (2005) *The CSIRO Total Wellbeing Diet*. Melbourne: CSIRO, Penguin.

8   DRUG THERAPY

Until relatively recently, the first choice antihypertensives were dictated by the old evidence base. This produced first-line therapy of β-blocker-thiazide combinations for all who could tolerate it. Successful trials with newer agents produced the ABCD rule, intellectually justified by combining drugs that worked on the RAAS with those that did not. However, since ASCOT, it has been widely accepted that β-blockers should lose their place as first-line drugs, and the rule has become the ACD rule (Figure 8.1). The simple operation of this gives ACEIs (or ARB if intolerant) as first-line drugs to all under 55, and those in special subgroups. The rationale

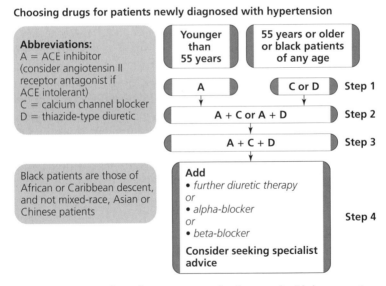

Choosing drugs for patients newly diagnosed with hypertension

Figure 8.1   Choosing drugs for patients newly diagnosed with hypertension. National Institute for Health and Clinical Excellence (2006). *CG34 Hypertension: management of hypertension in adults in primary care.* London: NICE. Available at www.nice.org.uk/CG34. Reproduced with permission.

for this is that such patients are more likely to have RAAS-responsive hypertension. Above 55, the first line is either a diuretic or a CCBD, depending upon individual clinical consideration. Failure of monotherapy causes addition of a drug from the other side of the algorithm. Further failure causes addition of the third drug. After this, specialist advice is recommended. Note that in several recent trials, the average number of medications required to achieve target blood pressure was three.

One of the more significant but unsung papers on hypertension is the Health Technology Assessment from 2003 (Box 8.1). This large meta-analysis of different drug groups showed that all antihypertensives are roughly equivalent in effectiveness, and that all are marketed at or near the upper end of their dose–response curve (Table 8.1). Titrating up dose schedules did not reduce blood pressure to a significant extent. It also showed that the side-effect profiles of drugs are sharply dose-dependent, except for ACEIs and ARBs. Combining two or three drugs at half-standard to standard doses is much more efficient, as the side-effects are not cumulative across group. Thus combination therapy at half standard to standard dose produces effective blood pressure lowering, broadly the same reduction in endpoints with better tolerability and fewer side-effects (Table 8.2). Note that there was insufficient trial evidence at the time of this analysis to include the α-blocker doxazosin in the analysis.

The practical effects of these two papers are straightforward. There is no rationale for titrating up monotherapy of CCBDs, diuretics or β-blockers; the side-effects increase sharply for little in the way of extra blood pressure reduction. There is some justification for titrating ACEIs and ARBs; there is modest further antihypertensive effect, but no increase in side-effects (cough is not dose-dependent). There is no data on doxazosin, the

---

Box 8.1 Meta-analysis of 354 trials

- Law *et al.*, *Health Technology Assessment*, and *BMJ*, 2003
- 40 000 treated patients, 16 000 placebo
- BP reductions singly and in combination, versus placebo
- Dose dependency
- Side-effects
- Average starting BP 154/97 mmHg

Table 8.1 Average BP reductions

Drug	Fall in BP
Thiazides	8.8/4.4
β-Blockers	9.2/6.7
ACEIs	8.5/4.7
ARBs	10.3/5.7
CCBDs	8.8/5.9

ACEI, Angiotensin converting enzyme inhibitor;
ARB, angiotensin receptor blocker;
CCBD, calcium channel blocking drug.

Table 8.2 Efficacy of drug combinations at half dose and full dose

	Number of drugs		
	1	2	3
BP reductions	6.7/3.7	13.3/7.3	19.9/10.7
Full dose	*9.0/4.7*	*17.2/8.9*	*24.7/12.6*
Reduction in stroke (%)	29 *32*	49 *52*	63 *65*
Reduction in IHD events	19 *20*	34 *34*	46 *45*

Figures in italics are for full dose
IHD, Ischaemic heart disease.

α-blocker. Therefore, in our clinic, we advocate the application of the ACD rule and the titration of the A component only. The same rationale underpins the use of fixed-dose combinations. Preparations that combine A+C or A+D (see Figure 8.1) can be used, with the manufacturers producing a range of doses of the A component, and the same dose of C or D.

The drugs in common usage are reviewed, in alphabetical order, in Table 8.3. The list of pros and cons contains the main clinical indications and contraindications. The contraindications marked with an asterisk should not be disregarded without specialist input.

Table 8.3 can be used with the ACD algorithm (see Figure 8.1). Non-dihydropyridine CCBDs should be reserved for difficult cases that are intolerant of dihydropyridines. ARBs are useful if there is an ACEI cough, or for 'ACEI escape'. If a patient is intolerant of any one of the ACD triad, I replace this with the α-blocker, unless there is a marked postural drop. Note that patients who have ankle swelling with a CCBD will often find that it improves when an ACEI or ARB is added. The relative venous dilatation of the CCBD is offset to some extent by the relative arterial dilatation of the A-type drug.

Table 8.3 Drugs in common usage

Drug	Pros	Cons
ACEIs	Left ventricular dysfunction, heart failure Post-myocardial infarction Stroke and post-stroke Diabetes Nephropathy, proteinuria	Cough (5%, not dose dependent) Renal impairment Renal artery disease Pregnancy*
ARBs	As for ACEI In ACEI intolerance	As for ACEI* Cough (1%, not dose dependent)
α-Blocker	Titratable Treats benign prostatic hypertrophy	Postural hypotension Heart failure
β-Blocker	Angina Post-myocardial infarction Heart failure	Diabetes Obesity Heart failure PAD Asthma, COPD* Heart block*
CCBDs (dihydropyridines)	Elderly ISH Angina	Ankle swelling Flushing
CCBDs (rate limiting)	Elderly ISH Angina	Constipation (verapamil) Heart failure Heart block* Combined with β-blocker*
Thiazide	Elderly ISH Heart failure Stroke prevention	Gout Hypokalaemia Combined with β-blocker

ACEI, Angiotensin converting enzyme inhibitor; ARB, angiotensin receptor blocker; CCBD, calcium channel blocker drug; COPD, chronic obstructive pulmonary disease; ISH, isolated systolic hypertension; PAD, peripheral arterial disease.
*Contraindications that should not be disregarded without specialist input.
Cough data from Pylypchuk GB. (1998) *Ann Pharmacother* **32**: 1060–66; and Israili ZH, Hall WD. (1992) *Ann Intern Med* **117**: 234–42.

Add-on drugs

Although adding further drugs is usually the prerogative of the specialist, there are occasional patients who are intolerant of two drugs out of the three ACD. As well as α-blockers, other useful drugs include spironolactone, the newer vasodilating β-blockers, and centrally acting drugs such as moxonidine.

Referral

If a patient cannot be controlled with three drugs, with one of these an A-type drug titrated to maximum dose, then specialist review should be sought. Other tripwires for onward referral include a rise in U/Es (or fall in eGFR) on ACEIs/ARBs, clinical markers of complex disease, and suspicion or detection of a renal, endocrine or neuro-endocrine pathology.

Antiplatelet therapy

Antiplatelet drugs should be offered to anyone on antihypertensive therapy over the age of 50, once their blood pressure is controlled, unless they have a bleeding diathesis, or develop dyspepsia on the drug. The usual dose is aspirin 75 mg once daily. Patients who are aspirin intolerant can try clopidogrel. This is more expensive than aspirin; a cost-effectiveness case can be made for its use in diabetics with established atherothrombotic disease. If it is regarded as mandatory that a patient take an antiplatelet agent despite dyspepsia or an ulcer history (for example, after repeat TIAs), then a proton pump inhibitor (PPI) should be given as well.

Lipid-lowering therapy

Lipid-lowering drugs should be offered to anyone on antihypertensive therapy over the age of 50 who has a total cholesterol greater than 5. The target cholesterol is less than 5, unless the patient is diabetic or has overt cardiovascular disease, in which case the target is probably 4.

Key points

- The old ABCD rule is now the ACD rule.
- Patients under 55 should be started on an A drug, which can be titrated.
- Patients over 55 should be started on C or D, with addition of a drug from the opposite side as the next step.
- Titrating most drugs increases the side-effect profiles without much additional increase in antihypertensive action.
- This, however, does not apply to ACEIs and ARBs, which can be titrated to maximal dose.
- In practice, patients are therefore treated with a fixed dose of C- or D-type drug with up-titration of the A-type drug.
- The cough side-effect of ACEIs (5%) and ARBs (1%) is not dose dependent.
- If patients are intolerant of any one of the A, C or D group of drugs, these can be replaced in the algorithm with an α-blocker, avoiding β-blockers where possible.
- Compliance is always an issue to be considered in refractory hypertension.
- Failure of control with the ACD three-drug combination is an indication for onward referral and/or more investigation.
- Antiplatelet drugs should be considered if tolerated and once the blood pressure is under control.
- In the context of global risk, most hypertensive patients should also be offered lipid-lowering therapy.

References and further reading

Higgins B et al. NICE CG34 (2006) Hypertension: management of hypertension in adults in primary care. Available at nice.org.uk, as the full guideline and as a quick reference guide.

Law M, Wald N, Morris J. (2003) Lowering blood pressure to prevent myocardial infarction and stroke: a new preventative strategy. Health Technol Assess 7(31). (Read summary for main points)

Wald N, Law M. (2003) A strategy to reduce cardiovascular disease by more than 80%. BMJ 326, 1419.

9 HYPERTENSION AND TREATMENT IN SUBGROUPS

Young hypertensives

Hypertension is uncommon in children, and usually represents an underlying pathology, with renal disease, malignancy and arteritic diseases the commonest causes. In children aged under 12, the Korotkov IV is usually used, converting to Korotkov V at 13. Paediatric hypertension is a specialised area, outside the consideration of this book. Diet and lifestyle factors are addressed, and the first-line therapies are the same as for adults.

Hypertension as a young adult often has an apparent precipitant, such as the OCP, or analgesic use after trauma. It is a moot point whether this represents a proximate cause, or an unmasking of an underlying tendency. If removal of the precipitant does not normalise blood pressure, then treatment is started. Some young hypertensives will 'reset', and stay normotensive when therapy is discontinued after a trial period. Those who do not, require further investigation. The current pragmatic view is to extend this approach to all under the age of 35.

Younger hypertensives are more likely to have a high RAAS driving their blood pressure. Therefore ACEIs (and ARBs) are the drugs of choice. These drugs are also relatively clean (apart from cough), and unlikely to interfere with lifestyle (social, sporting and sexual activities).

Pregnancy

Many pregnant women do not have a pre-conception blood pressure reading. The problem therefore is knowing who was normotensive pre-pregnancy, and who was not. For this reason, the term pregnancy-induced hypertension is falling out of favour. Instead it is better to consider hypertension in pregnancy on either side of the 20-week mark.

Prior to this, hypertension probably represents a chronic picture, whether previously recognised or not. After 20 weeks, there is the obvious clinical emergency of full-blown eclampsia. The various degrees of hypertension that fall short of this dramatic picture represent one of the following: chronic hypertension (previously unknown), mild, non-proteinuric pre-eclampsia, proteinuric pre-eclampsia, and pre-eclampsia complicating chronic hypertension. A blood pressure check 6 weeks post-partum should be normal in pre-eclampsia; persisting hypertension is indicative of previously unknown chronic hypertension.

Women with known hypertension pre-pregnancy should have carefully planned pregnancies, with weekly blood pressure measurements and assessments for intrauterine growth retardation (IUGR). Treatment can be optimised; though there is little evidence that this protects against pre-eclampsia, it is reasonable to expect this approach to minimise other potential problems. Note that the first-choice antihypertensives for young women (ACEIs, ARBs) are contraindicated in pregnancy.

There is little clear evidence for specific antihypertensives through pregnancy. Based on experience, there is a natural preference for older drugs, such as methyldopa and labetalol. Both of these can cause fatigue. After informed discussion, some patients are also happy to take newer dihydropyridine calcium channel blockers, although there is most experience with nifedipine. Of the β-blockers, atenolol seems to be associated with IUGR; others may be less so, but are probably best avoided. Diuretics deplete intravascular volume; as this is already a problem in pre-eclampsia, these drugs should not be used. Doxazosin is theoretically safe but hasn't been tested; hydrallazine is used but causes postural hypotension. Management of these patients is best left to secondary care. Eclampsia and its acute management are outside the scope of this book, but emergency treatment in the community can be commenced with intravenous labetalol.

Ethnic groups

South Asians have a high incidence of the metabolic syndrome and are prone to this syndrome at lesser values of visceral obesity than Caucasians. The hypertension that they develop is usually part of this picture. Aggressive management of all aspects of global risk in these individuals is essential. This metabolic syndrome picture has a major effect on drug choice. It becomes imperative to try and avoid β-blockers in these patients. First-line therapy is often an ACEI or ARB, with subsequent CCBDs, diuretic, then α-blocker. Lipid-lowering therapy for the atherogenic lipid profile is also very important.

Afro-Caribbeans have low plasma renin and aldosterone levels for a given blood pressure, compared to Caucasians. They respond better to salt restriction, and less well to ACEIs, ARBs and β-blockers. They may also have an increased incidence of angio-oedema with ACEIs. Treatment is usually commenced with a diuretic, with add-on drugs being CCBDs and then an α-blocker.

Diabetes

Broadly speaking, diabetes is now regarded as a cardiovascular disease equivalent. The JBS2 guidelines no longer contain diabetic charts, as it is assumed that diabetics over the age of 40 will automatically qualify for aggressive risk factor management. In fact, the incidence of hypertension in type 1 diabetics is the same as the general population, but the adoption of the more aggressive targets commits many of them to therapy. Type 2 diabetics are usually obese and have developed the disease as an extension of metabolic syndrome. The incidence of hypertension in this group is high, twice that of non-diabetics, as are the clustered risk factors of dyslipidaemia and visceral obesity. This has an impact on antihypertensive therapy choice.

In effect, all diabetics are regarded as being aged under 55 (in terms of the ACD rule), and are commenced on ACEIs (or ARBs if intolerant) as first-line therapy. Polypharmacy is usually dictated by the lower blood pressure targets for these patients. CCBDs and diuretics are added on. Unless there is angina, β-blockers should be avoided. Postural hypotension should be checked, especially if an α-blocker is to be used. Centrally acting drugs may feature earlier than in other treatment regimens. This is covered in more detail in Chapter 5.

Renal impairment

Renal disease can cause hypertension, and hypertension can cause renal disease. There is good evidence that, whatever the pathology of the renal impairment, good blood pressure control can delay progression, and reduce proteinuria. It is worth remembering that, given effective renal replacement therapy, most end-stage renal disease patients die from an accelerated atherothrombosis, usually cardiac or cerebrovascular. Even transplantation does not fully reverse this trend, and many transplanted patients remain or become hypertensive. The more aggressive targets of secondary prevention are routinely adopted by nephrologists.

Many renal patients cannot tolerate RAAS drugs without further deterioration in GFR. This may be acceptable in some cases, and is less important in those actually on renal replacement therapy. Transplanted patients may have a functional renal artery stenosis to the graft. In general, these considerations demote RAAS drugs to fourth or even fifth place in these patients. Instead, CCBDs, diuretics, α-blockers and centrally acting agents are chosen.

Overt cardiovascular disease

There are three groups to consider: ischaemic heart disease, cerebrovascular disease and peripheral arterial disease.

Ischaemic heart disease (IHD)

This group of patients will often have angina, and may have rhythm problems, particularly atrial fibrillation. This is the only group in which the advantages of β-blockade outweigh the disadvantages, and these drugs are first line. CCBDs should be long-acting (either by inherent pharmacokinetics or by preparation); rate-limiting CCBDs (verapamil, diltiazem) should be reserved for those intolerant of β-blockers. ACEIs and ARBs have additional protective effects, and indeed may be given in the absence of hypertension in patients with LVF or after a myocardial infarction (MI); the evidence for this is stronger for some drugs in this class than for others.

Cerebrovascular disease

This group of patients includes those with TIAs, atherothrombotic cerebrovascular accident (CVA) and haemorrhagic CVA. Since β-blockers reduce cerebral blood flow, they are best avoided unless there is concomitant angina (and even then, a rate-limiting CCBD might be better). There is good evidence for the use of certain ACEIs in this group of patients, even in the absence of hypertension. The lower, more aggressive blood pressure targets should be adopted – and possibly lower still, for cerebral haemorrhage patients. CCBDs may improve cerebral ischaemia. There is trial evidence in favour of indapamide. Thus patients are often treated with a combination of ACEI, diuretic and CCBD.

The most difficult clinical issue is how to manage hypertension in the immediate post-stroke period. A short period of raised blood pressure, up to 48 hours, seems to be some sort of injury response. Lowering blood pressure early can reduce cerebral perfusion, and possibly may extend the area of ischaemic damage into the surrounding penumbra of 'stunned' but still viable brain. On the other hand, hypertension can contribute to further bleeding in cerebral haemorrhage, and possibly to haemorrhagic conversion of atherothrombotic stroke. Finally, there is a later phase mortality in stroke, both from second events, and from other cardiovascular causes. There are ongoing trials in this area; what follows is as yet just opinion-based. Cerebral haemorrhage should be treated with prompt blood pressure lowering, using CCBDs at the core of the regimen; the risk of further bleeding seems higher than the perfusion injury risk. Atherothrombotic stroke should have the commencement of an ACEI/diuretic/CCBD regimen for hypertension 48–72 hours after the event. Uncontrolled hypertension immediately after atherothrombotic stroke should be treated cautiously with small dose increments of CCBD. The definition of 'uncontrolled' is debated, with some authors treating systolic values of 180, and others 220 mmHg. The lower value is used in local practice.

Peripheral arterial disease (PAD)

The significance of PAD as a marker for generalised atherothrombotic disease is still undervalued in routine clinical practice. But patients with PAD have significant 5-year morbidity and mortality from cardiovascular disease, and should be treated to aggressive risk modification targets. This treatment can also improve clinical presentation. PAD patients with hypertension have a significant incidence of renal artery stenosis. This does not preclude ACEIs and ARBs, but they must be used with caution, with recheck U/Es (and eGFR) 7–10 days after commencement. CCBDs are first line, and may also provide some symptom improvement. Diuretics are generally neutral. Although many PAD patients have covert IHD, β-blockers can worsen peripheral symptoms, and are once again demoted; if they must be used, the newer vasodilating β-blockers should be tried. The sequence of drugs is therefore CCBD, diuretic, ACEI/ARB with caution, then α-blocker or vasodilating β-blocker.

Acute (malignant) hypertension

This is a medical emergency, and should always be treated on an in-patient basis. Generally it is diagnosed on the basis of a diastolic BP of greater than 120 mmHg, and the presence of severe hypertensive retinopathy – flame haemorrhages, multiple exudates, papilloedema. The presence or absence of renal impairment, proteinuria and encephalo-pathy are all complicating features, but don't alter initial management. Despite the presentation, no underlying cause is found in two-thirds of patients. The majority of the rest will have renovascular or renal disease – neuro-endocrine causes are still rare, and Conn's syndrome even more so. Nonetheless, all malignant-phase hypertensives must be investigated for these conditions.

The key to management is not to drop the blood pressure too quickly. Sudden pressure drops will defeat the brain's autoregulatory response and cause cerebral infarction. The target is to reduce diastolic blood pressure by 25%, and to no lower than 100, in the first 48 hours. Thereafter, a fur-ther gradual reduction to target pressures can be achieved over several days. Intravenous and sublingual regimens have no place in the manage-ment of this condition, except in the very rare circumstances of encephalopathy removing oral compliance.

There are a number of drugs to avoid in malignant hypertension. ACEIs/ARBs can produce catastrophic falls in BP in those with renal and renovascular disease, where the presentation is being driven by the RAAS. Unopposed β-blockers can cause hypertensive crises in undiagnosed phaeochromocytomas, and must not be used unless this pathology has been ruled out. In theory, it is possible to give separate α- and β-blockade therapy to avoid this, namely doxazosin and (say) atenolol. However, from experience it is unwise to uncouple the two, in case of drug error, and the combined α,β-blocker labetalol is to be preferred. Diuretic therapy causes volume depletion; many malignant hypertensives are already volume depleted, and diuretics can then cause uncontrolled pressure drop, and also worsen renal impairment. Sublingual nifedipine is very erratically absorbed, and should be avoided.

This condition is therefore best treated initially with a short-acting CCBD, namely oral nifedipine, with additional oral labetalol as required. In the absence of labetalol, oral doxazosin can be used on its own. Investigation for the causes of hypertension are undertaken as in Chapter 6, but more expeditiously. Conventional target blood pressures are initially ignored. Close out-patient monitoring is required in the first few weeks after discharge, and targets achieved only gradually, once the initial phase of control is stabilised.

Key points

These are not summarised for this chapter; the specifics for each condition should be read under each subheading.

Further reading

Yip G, Hall J. (2007) *Comprehensive Hypertension*. Mosby.

10 REFRACTORY HYPERTENSION

For the purposes of this chapter, this is taken to represent any patient uncontrolled on three drugs, with one of these (usually the ACEI or ARB) titrated to maximum.

Non-compliance

Sadly this is one of the commonest causes of refractory hypertension. Careful and non-confrontational exploration of this topic may reveal the problem. Tablet counts and the conversion of prescriptions in pharmacies can help. Non-compliance is not just non-adherence to a drug regimen, but may also represent relaxation of some previous lifestyle restrictions. If a patient is on an ACEI, then their serum ACE level should be undetectable. If all else fails, a short in-patient stay can reveal the problem, with nurse administration of medication.

ACEI escape

As discussed in the earlier chapter, the other enzymes that convert ATI to ATII can upregulate when ACE is blocked. This can be sufficient to cause the BP to rise after initial control on an ACEI. The treatment is to reduce the ACEI dose by one increment, and add a low dose of ARB. The U/Es should be checked prior to this manoeuvre, and again 7–10 days later. An alternative is a small dose of spironolactone (12.5 mg, or 25 mg on alternate days), with the same check on renal function.

Pregnancy

This should always be considered in women of child-bearing age, and formally tested if necessary.

Missed pathology

A patient with uncontrolled hypertension despite compliance should always be considered for repeat investigation. Renal, renovascular, endocrine and neuro-endocrine causes all have to be revisited.

Renal pathology, if missed, is usually obvious at second look. Polycystic kidneys in obese patients can sometimes be missed on ultrasound. Analgesic nephropathy can show an evolving scan appearance with papillary necrosis.

Isotope renograms have a small but defined false-negative rate for renal artery stenosis, especially for bilateral disease. Or the patient may have developed an aggressive renal artery stenosis. An MR renal angiogram can be helpful.

Repeat urine collections can miss a phaeochromocytoma; a chromogranin A blood test can sometimes take matters further. If the clinical index of suspicion is sufficiently high, then neuro-endocrine tissue often 'lights up' with gadolinium contrast on MR scanning, or with radioisotope scanning (MIBG, octreotide).

Is the patient Cushingoid? Or acromegalic?

Is the low potassium just due to the diuretic? Or to Conn's syndrome?

Has the patient developed arthritis, or some other autoimmune disease?

It is often rewarding to reconsider the more unusual diagnoses under these circumstances, such as partial enzyme deficiencies in the adrenal glands, and juxtaglomerular apparatus tumours.

Exogenous drugs

Many patients take drugs of which we are not aware, and which can affect blood pressure. This can be as prosaic as over-the-counter anti-inflammatories, but the list includes caffeine and taurine stimulants (tablets or drinks), sodium-rich antacids, cough medicines, liquorice extracts, and various herbal preparations (particularly from Chinese or Indian practitioners). Some young women will obtain the combined OCP from a family planning service. Older women may take quite high doses of phyto-oestrogens. Young men may take anabolic steroids. Lastly, many recreational drugs have an adverse effect on blood pressure, particularly cocaine, amphetamine and their derivatives.

...And finally

Think about compliance again.

Key points

- Non-compliance must always be considered amongst the causes.
- Serum ACE levels should be undetectable in patients on ACEIs.
- ACEI escape can be treated by reducing the ACEI dose and adding a small dose of ARB (monitoring the U/Es carefully).
- It is always worth enquiring about non-prescribed drug intake.
- Some causative pathologies can be missed at first look, or can develop aggressively, and re-investigation should be considered.
- Pregnancy testing may be worthwhile.

Further reading

Alper AB, Calhoun DA. (1999) Contemporary management of refractory hypertension. *Curr Hypertens Rep* **1**(5), 402–407.
(Not that contemporary now, but still a useful overview)

11 PRACTICAL POINTS

This chapter contains a number of specific practical points from the other chapters, in alphabetical order.

ACEI escape

Blocking the conversion of angiotensinogen to angiotensin II by ACE inhibition leaves the possibility of upregulation of other pathways that effect this conversion, particularly via tissue plasminogen activator (tPA). In some patients this occurs at a sufficient rate to create a clinical problem. It does not necessarily mean a fall-off in compliance. The treatment is to reduce the ACEI by one dose increment and add an ARB at low dose, watching renal function carefully whilst doing so.

ACD rule

This has replaced the ABCD rule, relegating β-blockers to a distant fourth in the scheme of drug additions. The British Hypertension Society flow chart (see Figure 8.1) should be followed for all hypertensives in the first instance, only departing from this if there is some clinical override.

ABPM

Ambulatory blood pressure monitoring is a useful tool in dissecting out white coat effect, assessing true 24-hour blood pressure, and pointing up a lack of nocturnal dip. This last is an early predictor, and often seen in diabetic patients. Remember that an ABPM should read at least 10/5 mmHg lower than a casual office reading, and set the machine levels accordingly.

Antiplatelet therapy

This is an essential part of managing global risk. Although aspirin is not a benign drug, it should be used in hypertensive patients to further reduce the risk of thromboembolic disease, particularly stroke. In practice it is usually restricted to patients over 50 (and in whom the risk threshold of ≥20% is exceeded), those who already have atherothrombotic disease, and younger diabetics on other guardian medication. The dose of aspirin is 75 mg daily. Interestingly, clopidogrel is more effective in diabetic patients; its use becomes a matter for pharmaco-economics.

Blood pressure targets

From the JBS2 Guidelines:

- audit standard <150/90 mmHg
- optimal treatment standard <140/85 mmHg
- audit standard for diabetes <145/85 mmHg
- optimal treatment standard for diabetes and for high CVD risk <130/80 mmHg.

Combination therapy

The rationale for combination therapy is to reduce tablet count in patients on more complex drug regimens. Together with once-daily dosing, this has been proven to improve compliance. There is a good scientific basis for combining drugs from either side of the standard algorithm, particularly as the C/D drug is not titrated, and so only the dose of the A drug needs to be varied. A+D tablets are already commonplace, and an A+C combination has just been launched. The traditional pharmacologist's objections to these combinations is overcome by the therapeutic rationale and titration strategy. In addition, the non-titrated component (C or D) is often included at no extra cost.

Compliance

Always the elephant in the corner of the room in any discussion of uncontrolled blood pressure, this is notoriously difficult to confirm. As more polypharmacy is needed, this becomes more of a problem. If a patient is taking an ACEI, then their serum ACE levels should be undetectable.

Other than this, the only way to guarantee compliance is by admission and in-patient administration of medication. This is occasionally required to prove the point, both to patients and to other clinicians.

Cough

The incidence of cough is around 5% with ACEIs, and 1% with ARBs. If it is mandatory that one or other of these drugs be used, and cough is troublesome, it can sometimes respond to the use of nedocromil or similar inhalers. There is presumably some effect in reducing kinin release. This is an off-licence use for these inhalers, probably best left to a hospital specialist for initiation.

Diabetes

Regarded as a cardiovascular disease equivalent, the presence of diabetes mandates aggressive risk factor reduction, tighter targets, and the use of guardian medication in all over 40. This will consign some low-risk, well-controlled type 1 diabetics to medication, but this is justifiable in (diabetic) population terms. In terms of hypertension, the trials generate a strong bias to using ACEIs (or ARBs in intolerant patients) for renal protection. The target for diabetes control *per se* is HbA1c <6.5%.

ECG

Despite the false-negative rate for LVH, an ECG should still be performed on any individual being considered for antihypertensive therapy. If LVH is suspected despite a 'normal' ECG, an echocardiogram for left ventricular mass may help.

Education

This is self-evident. Patients who are educated in their disease and its management are more likely to comply with long-term drug therapy. Both the British Hypertension Society (at http://www.bhsoc.org) and the Blood Pressure Association (at http://www.bpassoc.org.uk) have patient information websites and leaflets.

Global risk

Although this is a short book on hypertension, it is important to place the treatment of blood pressure in the context of global risk, both of the individual and in population terms. Various risk-calculating algorithms are available – consistency is the key, with the risk score used and its value recorded.

Hypertensive crisis

Defined as a diastolic BP of >120, with accompanying retinal signs, this is a medical emergency and requires prompt admission. In the community, the only therapy that can safely be started (whilst waiting for transport to the hospital) is an oral (**not** sublingual) CCBD – nothing else is safe in this setting.

HRT

This is a contentious area, with new data still emerging. At present, HRT cannot be recommended for the purposes of ameliorating cardiovascular risk. If an individual wishes to take HRT for other reasons, they can be reasonably confident that there is a low risk attached to this for the first 5 years of therapy, both in terms of cardiovascular disease and for cancer (unless there is a family history of breast cancer).

JBS2

The Joint British Societies' Guidelines on Prevention of Cardiovascular Disease in Clinical Practice is published in *Heart* **91**(suppl V), December 2005. This is available as a reprint or on line at http://www.heartjnl.com; this is compulsory reading in the field.

Lipids

A full lipid profile is mandatory in the management of cardiovascular risk. The Heart Protection Study has placed emphasis on treating this part of the risk profile reasonably aggressively in hypertensive patients. As LDL is the primary target, generic statin use is first line, unless the triglycerides are markedly elevated.

Lipid-lowering therapy

Lipid-lowering drugs should be offered to anyone on antihypertensive therapy over the age of 50, who has a total cholesterol >5. The target cholesterol is less than 5, unless the patient is diabetic or has overt cardio-vascular disease, in which case the target is probably 4.

Lipid targets

From the JBS2 Guidelines:

- audit standard total cholesterol <5.0 mmol/l
- optimal treatment standard total cholesterol <4.0 mmol/l
- audit standard calculated LDL cholesterol <3.0 mmol/l
- optimal treatment standard calculated LDL cholesterol <2.0 mmo/l.

There are no current standards for HDL and triglycerides. Best practice suggests triglycerides <1.7 mmol/l and HDL >1.3 mmol/l, but these are not evidence-based.

Metabolic syndrome

Diagnosed by waist measurements, this is a powerful predictor of cardio-vascular risk, which is at very nearly the same level as diabetes. Recording BMI and waist measurement is an important part of risk management.

Critical waist measurements are:

- male Caucasian >102 cm (40 in)
- male Asian >90 cm (35.5 in)
- female Caucasian >88 cm (34.5 in)
- female Asian >80 cm (31.5 in).

Note the ethnic differences; Asians are more prone to metabolic syndrome at lower absolute levels of visceral obesity.

The metabolic syndrome has been defined recently as three of the following:

- increased waist measurement, as above
- elevated triglycerides >1.7 mmol/l
- decreased HDL <1.03 mmol/l for men, <1.29 mmol/l for women
- BP >130/85 or active blood pressure lowering therapy
- fasting plasma glucose >5.6 mmol/l or active blood glucose lowering therapy.

Remember that the natural progression of untreated metabolic syndrome is to develop overt type 2 diabetes.

Peripheral arterial (obstructive) disease (PAD)

PAD is the poor relation of atherothrombotic diseases, but merits aggressive therapy, both of itself and as a marker for early cardiovascular events. It is also associated with a high incidence of renal artery stenosis. This does not preclude the use of ACEIs/ARBs in this group, but care should be taken with renal function.

Pregnancy

New hypertension in pregnancy is managed with rather old-fashioned drugs because of their safety profile. See the specifics outlined in Chapter 10.

Renal impairment

This both increases the cardiovascular risk of the individual and reduces the therapeutic options. However, most patients with modest impairment by eGFR can tolerate ACEIs and ARBs, though careful monitoring is required. The question of diagnosing renal impairment by eGFR alone is difficult, and still under review.

Salt

Reducing salt intake is an important part of the non-pharmacological treatment of blood pressure, and it is worth discussing the hidden levels of salt in prepared foods and in beer, as well as the more obvious crisps and snacks.

SIGN guidelines

The Scottish Intercollegiate Guideline Network (SIGN) is an independent guideline organisation. Its output is produced by rigorous review of published evidence, which occasionally produces anomalies compared to other guidelines. Cardiovascular disease risk estimation and prevention was published in February 2007. An implementation document accompanying this makes interesting reading, including a realistic estimate of costs.

Smoking

Smoking cessation is mandatory, though a non-confrontational approach is usually more productive. Self-cessation provides higher 1-year success rates than pharmacology support, but this should be offered where needed.

Spironolactone

The secret weapon. Adding 12.5 (half a tablet) to 25 mg once daily to a complex antihypertensive regimen can still reduce BP by as much as 20/10 in patients not on ACEIs/ARBs, and by 12/7 in those that are. This is an off-licence use of this drug. Care must be taken with renal function, and with gynaecomastia in males.

Target organ damage

This is important in stratifying risk; its presence commits the individual to tighter targets. An ECG, fundoscopy and urinalysis are mandatory.

Urinalysis

As part of the target organ damage screen, this should be performed on all patients being considered for therapy. If negative for proteinuria and haematuria, it should be rechecked for microalbuminuria (either by specialised stick test or with a laboratory specimen).

12 CONCLUSION

The practical management of hypertension encompasses:

- detecting the condition, both in those at high risk and in the more general population;
- screening for secondary causes of hypertension;
- giving diet, exercise, weight optimisation and lifestyle advice;
- treating with appropriate drugs and combinations;
- managing associated glucose handling disorders and the metabolic syndrome;
- placing the hypertension and the patient in the context of global risk;
- modifying and treating other facets of this global risk; and
- above all, explaining to the patient the lifetime effort that is required, with drug and lifestyle compliance.

This is no easy task, and is certainly beyond the realistic aspirations of a single consultation. It requires considerable resource, and although calculations about drug budgets abound, the main resource is that of the time commitment for the health-care professionals involved. The requirement to titrate drug therapy to response, to continuously reinforce lifestyle messages, and to monitor long-term, all place an additional burden on the system. But as we have an impact on the epidemiology of cardiovascular disease, with public health initiatives, education and medication, there will be a predictable health gain that is clearly worthwhile on even the meanest calculations. Imagine that there was an expensive but proven inoculation that, once given, deferred the onset of cardiovascular disease by 10–15 years. There would be a public outcry if it were not made widely available. Instead of the inoculation, there are a series of lifestyle, dietary and drug measures that require effort by both the patient and the professional. With commitment, care and compliance, we can reap the same reward.

Moving the mean population blood pressure value, and thereby moving its cardiovascular risk, is a mammoth task. There is, however, the medical and political will to achieve this. Archimedes stated that with a place to stand and a long enough lever he could move the world. I hope that this book adds a little strength to your arms.

Bonne chance, mes amis.

INDEX

Page numbers in *italics* refer to tables

78